The Walkers of Hanningfield

Surveyors and Mapmakers Extraordinary

The Walkers of Hanningfield

Surveyors and Mapmakers Extraordinary

by

A. C. Edwards and K. C. Newton

Buckland Publications Ltd.
125 High Holborn, London WC1V 6QA

ISBN 0 7212 0614 X

Printed and bound in Great Britain by
Buckland Press Ltd., Dover, Kent.

CONTENTS

MAP AND DIAGRAMS

PARISHES AND MANORS

PREFACE

This is a book which has had to wait a long time for publication, so much so that the chronology of events has become a little hazy. About 1969, the two authors began to work on it, intermittently, and they completed about 95% of it by 1972. They hoped to have it published by the Essex Record Office, but the high cost of printing an expensive book in times of financial stringency made this impossible. In 1975, John Thorpe of the Regency Press became deeply interested in the manuscript and its illustrations, but, again, high costs and economic blizzards, and notably the cut-back in grants to public and university libraries, prevented publication.

Then it became obvious that the illness which had afflicted one of the authors for some time was becoming increasingly worse; he died in March 1978. Meanwhile, the other author, who had also suffered a serious illness, entered his seventies and could not face the task of hawking the manuscript around the publishing world in a climate unfavourable to publishers.

However, late in 1981, John Thorpe, who had never lost his interest in the project, renewed his acquaintance with the manuscript, and in 1982 it was decided that the Buckland Press, now owner of the Regency Press, should publish it.

ACKNOWLEDGMENTS

A considerable debt is owed to Brian Smith, a former colleague and now Secretary to the Historical Manuscripts Commission. In the early 1960s he became interested in the Walker family. He consulted nearly a hundred original medieval and later documents and a number of secondary sources, and in 1965 he produced 23 typed foolscap pages of notes. These he most generously handed over to the two authors. They proved invaluable, and pointed the way to further research into the Walker family background.

Other friends and former colleagues have also been most helpful. Victor Gray, the present Essex County Archivist, very kindly catalogued those Walker maps which had been deposited in the Essex Record Office since Kenneth Newton's death, skilfully following the form used in the Chronological Catalogue; and in many other ways he has taken a close interest in the production of the book. My wife, Nancy Briggs, Senior Assistant Archivist at the Essex Record Office, has read the script and made a number of valuable suggestions; she has also proof-read and checked the book at all stages of its production. John McCann has kindly read Chapter Four and has made very helpful comments. His colleagues in the Buildings and Conservation Section of the Essex County Planning Department have readily given advice on matters relating to vernacular buildings. Mildred Newton, Kenneth Newton's widow, has patiently typed all the amendments needed in the later stages of production; the original text had been typed by Ken Newton himself. The greater part of the tribute to Kenneth Newton is taken from the obituary written by my wife and published in the *Transactions of the Essex Archaeological Society;* it is reproduced here by the Society's permission—and hers.

Throughout the years, the Essex County Visual and Aural Aids Service and particularly, R. W. Bates and D. Tobias, have always been ready and willing to help members of the Essex Record Office. I am most grateful for their invaluable skill and advice.

I should like to thank all owners of Walker maps and surveys for their generosity and public spirit in depositing their archives with the Essex Record Office, and thereby making them available for research. Lord Petre, who has deposited six Walker maps and three written surveys, retains the Ingatestone map of 1605, by John Walker junior, in his own custody; this map, too, he has kindly allowed to be reproduced. Another map, the Terling map, 1597, is also in private custody; it is published by courtesy of the Hon. Guy Strutt. Four Walker maps are in public custody. The map of Little Leighs, 1609 (MDA 24), is reproduced by permission of the Public Record Office. The splendid map of Foxcott, Andover, 1614 (MS. Rolls, Hants 44), by John Walker junior, is reproduced by courtesy of the Curators of the Bodleian Library, Oxford. The photocopy of the missing map of Tolleshunt Darcy, 1616 (BL maps 2420(F)), and the map of High Easter, 1622 (Additional MS. 41848) are published by kind permission of the British Library.

A.C.E.

KENNETH CHARLES NEWTON
1927-1978

Ken Newton died on 16th March, 1978, after a long illness, borne with characteristic fortitude and quiet good humour.

He was an Essex man, brought up in West Ham and educated at Stratford Grammar School. After service in the Army Intelligence Corps, in 1948 he became a clerk in the Essex Record Office, to which he devoted the rest of his working life. He was promoted Assistant Archivist in 1954, becoming Senior Assistant Archivist in 1961. On the retirement of the first County Archivist, Dr. F. G. Emmison, in June 1969, he was appointed to succeed him, to the delight of his colleagues, who found him always ready to encourage them to pursue their own researches in local history. As County Archivist, he served on the Council of the Essex Archaeological Society and as Vice-Chairman of the Chelmsford Excavation Committee. Professionally, he was especially interested in the technical aspects of archive work: conservation, photography and publication. The photographic section has been of considerable aid to the other services provided by the Essex Record Office. He actively encouraged the public research facilities of the office, already highly developed during Dr. Emmison's time.

Following early work on 16th century manorial records, he was drawn towards the records of the medieval manor on which he became an acknowledged expert. In 1960, the Essex Record Office published *Thaxted in the Fourteenth Century,* a work which threw light both on the manor and the borough, and on the town's legendary cutlery industry. He himself saw his work on Thaxted as the first in a series of much-needed sample studies based on the medieval records of Essex manors. He next turned his attention to the ancient demesne manor of Writtle; the results of his research brought him academic recognition with the award of an M.A. degree in the Department of English Local History at Leicester University in 1967. Phillimore published *The Manor of Writtle: the development of a royal manor, c.1086-c.1500* in 1970. A pioneer article in the *Journal of the Society of Archivists,* vol. 3, No. 10 (October 1969), used Writtle records as 'A Source for Medieval Population Statistics'. At the time of his death, he was working on Hatfield Broad Oak, another ancient demesne manor.

He was a valuable and enthusiastic member of the team involved in the early exhibitions at Ingatestone Hall from 1954. He was responsible for two exhibition booklets: *Essex and the Sea,* 1959; *Medieval Essex,* 1962. As

County Archivist, he launched the series of Seax Teaching Portfolios, compiling *Highways and Byways* himself; and had high hopes for a series of 'Edited Texts'. His brief history of *Essex County Council, 1889-1974,* was compiled at the request of the Chairman of the old County Council. The passage of the Local Government Act, 1974, provided the opportunity to improve the service by the Essex Record Office by setting up a branch at Southend.

His enthusiasm for cartography led him to a deep knowledge of the subject. He prepared the entries for estate maps in the *First Supplement to the Catalogue of Maps* and took an increasing share in the *Second* and *Third Supplements.* His long-standing interest in the Elizabethan and Jacobean estate cartographers, John Walker, his son, John, and their kinsman, Samuel Walker, is reflected in his contribution to this book: he wrote the chapter on Draughtsmanship and Calligraphy and almost all of the Chronological Catalogue.

The Essex Branch of the Historical Association was fortunate in having Ken Newton successively as Honorary Secretary and Chairman. The Association published his *Medieval Local Records: a Reading Aid,* in 1971, with many Essex examples.

Never robust, his health began to deteriorate in 1971, compelling him to restrict many of his activities. Throughout this difficult period, he owed a great deal to the support of his wife, Mildred. His sudden death in 1978 occurred after a severe attack of influenza. He was already gravely ill when he tape-recorded a contribution to a week-end conference at Clacton, published in *Archaeology in Essex to A.D. 1500* (C.B.A. Research Report, No. 34); the volume is dedicated to his memory 'in recognition of the considerable assistance which he gave to Essex archaeologists during his years as the County Archivist'. Even in this short paper on the value of documentary evidence and maps, one can detect the dry humour with which he always tempered his considerable scholarship.

The memory of his life and work will always remain green in the minds of his friends. Nor will he be forgotten by a wider public: in 1978, the Chairman of Essex County Council agreed to revive the annual public lecture on some aspect of Essex history, which was to be known in future as the Newton Memorial Lecture in commemoration of his service as County Archivist. Appropriately, the first lecture, 'The Walkers of Hanningfield', was the subject of this book.

Distribution of Walker maps

INTRODUCTION

During the Elizabethan age, surveying and mapmaking changed rapidly from a very imperfect craft to an art form tempered by increasingly exact science. Many learned works have been written on this, and none more delightful and erudite than the essays of the late Edward Lynam.[1] Nowhere can this advance be better demonstrated than in the maps of the Walkers of Hanningfield.

Forty years ago, the Walkers had been sleeping in obscurity for over three centuries; their awakening underlines the value of local depositories. At the end of the Second World War, when the Essex Record Office was dealing with a renewed influx of records from many sources, it was realised that a corpus of outstanding Elizabethan and Jacobean estate maps by two gifted cartographers was gradually accumulating. The *Catalogue of Maps in the Essex Record Office, 1566-1860* (1947) states that the maps of the elder John Walker and his son John 'are a delight to the eye, are of absorbing interest and remarkable accuracy'. In the same year, Irvine Gray, soon to be County Archivist of Gloucestershire, contributed an important article to *Country Life*.[2] For some years this has remained the only detailed work in print on the Walkers, although reproductions of some of their maps, with comments, have appeared in Essex Record Office publications[3] and elsewhere.[4] In 1969 a lecture by one of the authors of this book was published in *The Bulletin of the Society of University Cartographers;*[5] it may be regarded as a curtain-raiser to the present volume.

It is almost a commonplace that maps seem to impose a magic spell on many people, not least on those who never use them in any professional sense. The One-Inch Ordnance Survey had that magnetic quality. Walker maps have it; they are compelling like the music of the Pied Piper. In the first instance, they attract by their colouring and their fine lettering and draughtsmanship; then they kindle confidence by their accuracy; then they bind the viewer to the performance of some particular task. The elder Walker's map of Chelmsford, 1591, committed Miss Hilda Grieve to the study of an Elizabethan town centre, and thence to studies of that town at other periods of its development.[6] One of the authors of this volume took one side of Ingatestone village street, as shown on the Walker map of 1601, and used it as a basis for a close study (never published) of every tenement and its occupants throughout the Elizabethan period. This study could well be extended backwards and forwards in time, since it so happens that the evidence in manorial records is virtually complete from 1279 and there are many other supporting documents. The other author, when compiling his book, *John Petre*, found the Walker maps of Petre family lands most helpful in understanding the social and economic background of John, 1st Lord Petre, and his household. Indeed, it is possible to go back again and again to Walker maps, as eminent scholars go back to Domesday Book, and still find something new. They will continue to offer exasperating conundrums to local historians. Will those maps of mid-Essex estates, for example, continue to yield more knowledge of ancient enclosure? Are some of the outbuildings depicted by the Walkers really medieval timber-framed kitchens, and will any of them be found to have survived? Why, in the middle of West Horndon Park, did John Walker the elder depict 'Mr. Wallgraves' Arbovr' (Plate X)? Was he Nicholas Waldegrave, Lady Petre's brother, or was he Charles, the other brother, and, anyhow, why did he need such solitude?

Unfortunately, far too little has emerged on the lives of the Walkers. Brian Smith's patient and extensive researches were continued by the authors, but the chapter on 'Family Background' still leaves a number of unsolved problems. The family home was Kent's Farm, West Hanningfield (Plate XXXIX), and although the elder Walker lived at Ballingdon-cum-Brundon on the Essex-Suffolk border around 1588,[7] there is little doubt that he and his son retained Kent's Farm and a close interest in West Hanningfield throughout their lives. Both were buried there, the son in 1618 and the father in 1626.[8] Still less is known about Samuel Walker, a third mapmaker of the family, inferior in craftsmanship to the others, but still good by Jacobean standards. It is not even certain how he fits into the family tree; the probability is that he was a nephew of the elder John.

A gratifying amount of the Walker legacy has survived. Twenty-two maps* and two written surveys with maps can be attributed to one or the other of the two Johns, or jointly to both. There are also five written surveys without maps; one is in the hand of John the younger; two were compiled by the Walkers but are not in the hand of either; two were not compiled by the Walkers but were intended to accompany Walker maps. Lastly, there is an early 18th century copy of a map now lost. Seventeen of these maps, the two surveys with maps and the five other surveys are deposited with the Essex Record Office. Two maps are still in private custody, another is in the Public Record Office, one is in the Bodleian Library and two (one of them surviving only in monochrome photographic form) are in the British Library. All maps and surveys are of Essex

---

*This number includes *S. Hanningfield, 1615*, which the late K. C. Newton eventually ascribed, very tentatively, to Samuel Walker (see Chronological Catalogue).

estates except that in the Bodleian; this is of Foxcott, near Andover, Hampshire, and was commissioned by an Essex landowner. Most of them relate to mid-Essex estates, ten of them to lands belonging to the Petre family. A few are unimportant; one is merely a draft map; a few, although now expertly repaired, are defective through earlier neglect. About ten maps can be described as splendid early examples of accurate surveying, skilled draughtsmanship and fine lettering.

Speculation on missing maps is scarcely profitable, unless their former existence is documented. There are sad gaps in the chronology, but the comforting probability is that the losses are fewer than the survivors. A map of Broomfield, c.1600, is thought to have been destroyed in the 1940s.[9] The absence of a map of the Manor of Writtle is most regrettable. It was royal demesne; its development was remarkable;[10] it was the most prized of the Petre lands; indeed, when Sir John Petre was raised to the peerage in 1603 he took his title not from West Horndon or Ingatestone, where his principal mansions lay, but from Writtle—he became Baron Petre of Writtle. The manor is still retained by the family. It is inconceivable that this jewel in the Petre coronet was not depicted by the Walkers while they were working for Sir John. Its date would probably have been in the late 1590s.

There is evidence of a survey, carried out by John Walker the elder, of which there is no trace. In a conveyance of the Manor of Sheriffs in Colne Engaine and Earls Colne, dated 11th June, 1604,[11] the respective acreages of the demesne and customary or copyhold lands are warranted in the following words, 'That the Demeasne Landes and Tenementes of the saide Mannour or Lordshipp doe conteyne and be Two hundred and Eleaven Acres And that the Customarie or Coppieholde Landes of the saide Mannour or Lordshipp doe Conteyne Fiftie and Seaven Acres and more, according as is specified in a certain survey thereof taken by John Walker Architecte on the Twentithe daie of October 1589 As by a note or wrightinge thereof made bearinge date the saide Twentithe day of October being subscribed by the said John Walker it maie appear.' It is clear that this was a written survey, probably brief in character, unaccompanied by a map.

Samuel Walker was a useful Jacobean estate cartographer, as good as Amyce, as good as the Treswells, but hardly the equal of Agas. His surveying was accurate; his execution was adequate, though a little undisciplined; his drawings of buildings (at least on four of his surveying maps) provide valuable guides to the study of vernacular architecture. But he was not a patch on his incomparable kinsman. Five of his maps and one written survey have survived; one map is in the British Library, the others are in the custody of the Essex Record Office. Four of the maps are signed;

the other has been tentatively attributed to him on stylistic and palaeographical grounds (see S. Hanningfield, 1615, in the Chronological Catalogue).

One other map (Mountnessing, 1622, by Andrew Pease) deserves to be included in this book, as it shows Walker influence. Pease was a trusted servant of the Petre family for over thirty years and would have known the Walkers well.

With two exceptions, the names of those who commissioned the surviving maps and surveys are known. It is difficult even to guess how John Walker the elder acquired his early patrons, notably Andrew Jenour of Dunmow and John Aylmer, Bishop of London, although Sir John Ive, who commissioned the Boxted survey of 1586, may have been related to the eminent mapmaker, Ralph Agas.

About 1590, a pattern of patronage begins to emerge. John Walker the elder was certainly well known to the estate cartographer, Israel Amyce (see chapter on 'Family Background'); indeed, he was probably Amyce's pupil. Amyce was a landowner and a justice of the peace in north Essex. Sir Thomas Mildmay and his close friend, Sir John Petre, dominated the Essex bench.[12] In 1589, Amyce and Walker were together in Chelmsford at the time of the Assize and Easter Quarter Sessions,[13] and in 1591 Walker's important maps of Mildmay's manors of Chelmsford and Moulsham appeared. It would seem highly probable that Mildmay recommended him to Petre, who became his most important patron. The Walkers were 'in'; their future patronage was assured. All subsequent patrons were members of the circle of central and mid-south Essex landowners, of whom at least five were justices of the peace; one, Stephen Beckingham, was the brother of a justice; Sir John Tyrell was a kinsman of Sir John Petre; and the Lords Bergavenny and Sussex had close ties with the Petre family.

While the greater part of this book was being written in the early 1970s, the authors were acutely conscious that Time was the enemy—time to unravel the documentary evidence, especially the internal evidence of maps; time to do enough of the vital fieldwork. Moreover, both authors, through serious illnesses, had unmistakable evidence of mortality. Limits had to be set to the scope of the book and the time to be spent on it. By 1972, as the Preface indicates, most of it was completed. Further study of the maps allied to more fieldwork may lead others to modify or extend some of the conclusions reached here; but perhaps sufficient has been done to show that the Walkers occupy a unique place in the story of early estate cartography. On one point the authors had always been confident: the illustrations will give pleasure to many people.

Addendum

Through Dr. G. Scurfield of Melbourne, Australia, the existence of another map by Samuel Walker has become known. It covers the demesne lands of the manor of Waltham Bury in Great Waltham, and is in the Devonshire Collections at Chatsworth. It was surveyed and executed in 1643 on behalf of Robert, Earl of Warwick. It is 34 inches by 29 inches and is drawn on parchment to a scale of 16 rods to the inch. Apart from light staining it is in good condition. Most of the lands depicted were in the occupation of Sir Richard Everard of Langleys, Great Waltham. Apart from Waltham Bury and its outbuildings, the only other buildings shown are Great Waltham church and Fitzjohn's farmhouse.

It is through the kindness of Mr. Michael Pearman, Librarian and Archivist at Chatsworth, that it has been possible to compile this note.

★ ★ ★

Since the *addendum,* above, was written in February 1984, another map by Samuel Walker has been found in the Manchester Collection in the Huntingdon branch of the Cambridgeshire County Record Office (Cat. No. M16/54). It is 21 by 17 inches and depicts the island of Havengore at the mouth of the Thames. It is entitled 'Haven Goere in no Parishe lying Butt neere Wakering magna, July 1645', and is signed by Samuel Walker. No scale is given. Its 180 acres of grazing land is surrounded by marshes, and is protected on the east and west by seawalls and on the north and south by ditches. The only building shown is a single-storeyed cottage. The island was in the occupation of Thomas Finche of Billericay; its ownership is not indicated, but it was undoubtedly part of the vast estates of Robert Rich, the eminent Earl of Warwick. The map is competently executed, but may have been no more than a draft. The existence of the map was kindly confirmed by Mr. Adrian Hill, the archivist in charge of the Huntingdon branch. There is a photostat copy in the custody of the Essex Record Office (Cat. No. T/M 503).

Before these two discoveries, it was known that Samuel Walker was alive in 1638, but he could not be traced beyond this date. The number of his surviving maps now stands at six; seven if the map of South Hanningfield, *c.* 1615, can be regarded as an early example of his work.

Notes and References

1. E.g. his book, *The Mapmaker's Art* (The Batchworth Press, 1953).
2. I. E. Gray, 'Maps of 350 Years Ago', *Country Life* (16th May, 1947).
3. K. C. Newton, *Medieval Essex* (Essex Record Office Publication, No. 36, 3rd imp., 1968); A. C. Edwards, *Essex Homes* (E.R.O. Pubn. No. 30, 3rd edn., 1969), *The Visual Arts in Essex* (E.R.O. Pubn. No. 50, 1969) and especially *Elizabethan Essex* (E.R.O. Pubn. No. 34, 4th imp., 1968) and *The Face of Essex* (E.R.O. Pubn. No. 46, 1967).
4. Especially A. L. Rowse, *The England of Elizabeth*, Vol. I, p.160 (Macmillan, 1950).
5. 'The Walkers of Essex', *Bulletin of the Society of University Cartographers*, Vol. 4, No. 1 (1969).
6. See f.n. 16 in chapter on 'The Value of Walker Maps as an Aid to the Study of Secular Buildings', p.95.
7. E.R.O., D/DP O6/12, 16.
8. D/P 247/1/1.
9. Ex. inf. Dr. F. G. Emmison.
10. K. C. Newton, *The Manor of Writtle* (Phillimore, 1970).
11. E.R.O., D/DSx 49.
12. Professor Joel Samaha's analytical table, printed as an appendix in F. G. Emmison's, *Elizabethan Life: Disorder* (E.R.O. Pubn. No. 56, 1970) shows that Sir Thomas Mildmay attended 92 sessions between 1569 and 1603, and Sir John Petre, 67 sessions between 1573 and 1603. The next highest figures were held by Mildmays—Thomas Mildmay of Springfield, 50, and Henry Mildmay, 43.
13. E.R.O., D/DP O6/15.
14. In the next generation, William, 2nd Lord Petre, bought the Hanningfield group of manors from Henry, 9th Lord Bergavenny; with the deeds and other muniments went two Walker maps and two Walker written surveys.

Walker Family Background

Through all the uncertainties which shroud the family background of the Walkers, one fact shines clearly—their home from the early 16th century to 1589 and again in the early 17th century, was Kent's Farm, West Hanningfield. It may even have been the Walker home continuously from c.1515 to the death of John Walker, the elder of the two great mapmakers, in 1626. It takes its name from the Kent family, first recorded in West Hanningfield in 1276.[1] By 1480 they were in posession of the house and its land,[2] which had earlier been known as Wyses Thaccher, probably after a John Wyse, thatcher.[3]

The home survives (Plate XXXIX). The Royal Commission says it was built probably in the 16th century.[4] It was a hall-house with a hall and one two-storeyed crosswing, but, as the Commission discovered, it is difficult to date closely because so much of the framework, including the timbers of both roofs, is completely covered. Almost certainly the hall-block was rebuilt in the 17th century, or at least had its roof raised. The crosswing is not later than c.1400, and may be earlier. Unfortunately, no Walker drawing of their home has survived. In three maps[5] they covered parts of the parish, but not this area, which lies about one mile west of the parish church.

The first of the Walkers to live at Kents was Thomas, possibly the son of George Walker who had been presented at the manor courts in 1507 and fined 4d as a common brawler.[6] About 1515,[7] Thomas Walker married Alice, daughter of William and Letitia Tabbard, tenants of Kents. When Tabbard died c.1514, Alice inherited one-third of Kents.[8] Later, in 1527, her husband, Thomas, was admitted to a second one-third.[9] In the court rolls, for the middle part of Henry VIII's reign his name appears fairly regularly, usually as chief pledge and a member of the homage.[10] He died in 1538; his son, John Walker, was declared his heir and admitted to one-third of Kents,[11] but he probably did not take possession until the second marriage of his mother, c.1545, to John Trewlove.[12]

This John Walker was a carpenter and a yeoman; he was the father of John the Architector (as he called himself), the elder of the two great mapmakers. John, the carpenter, first occurs in the West Hanningfield court rolls in 1534;[13] he was a member of the homage in every roll down to 1586, and he was elected constable in 1554.[14] He probably never left the village. He was married about 1550, or earlier. His wife's name was

Eleanor but her surname is not known; she was probably the 'mother' Walker who was buried at West Hanningfield in March 1589[15] about a month before his own death. He may well have been a churchwarden of West Hanningfield, concerned with the performance of parish plays, so popular in the Chelmsford area: in the Chelmsford Churchwardens' accounts for 1570, 16s.8d. was 'receyvd of John Walker of Hanfield for the heier of the players garments'.[16] In 1578 he surrendered Kents and its lands with the intention that the lord should regrant it to him and his wife for the term of their respective lives, with remainder to a Richard Bridges. It may never be known if Bridges acquired Kents in 1589; there is a gap in the court rolls from 1586 to 1592. What is certain is that John the Carpenter's son, John the Architector, appears fairly regularly in the court rolls from 1596 to 1601, and again from 1610 to 1625.[17] Moreover, in 1610, Margaret Wilkinson, widow, into whose ownership the house had come, was granted a licence to rent Kents to him for a term of 16 years.[18] Thus, Kents probably remained a Walker home until the Architector's death.

John, the carpenter, died almost certainly in 1589. His will[19] was made on 9th April, 1589, when he was 'sick of body'; it was proved at Chelmsford but no date is given. He left small sums of money to his grandchildren and other relations and the residue to his son, Cyprian, who succeeded him as carpenter. The overseers of his will were his other sons, John the Architector, and Richard.

John the Architector may always remain an enigmatic and obscure figure. Extensive searches have revealed a number of miscellaneous facts, but only four of these are really significant. He was born probably c.1550 perhaps a little earlier, certainly well before the West Hanningfield parish register which begins in 1558; but there are no records of him until his survey, with maps, of West Tilbury in 1584, when he was already a trained and skilled draughtsman, nearly but not quite at the height of his powers, reached in his map of Chelmsford, 1591. He was married probably between 1570 and 1575. The name of his wife is not known for certain, but most of the Walker women buried at West Hanningfield after 1575 can be accounted for until Lucy Walker, widow, who was buried in 25th October, 1627. This was 15 months after John's death and it seems likely that she was his widow.[20] Their son, John Walker, who became as great a mapmaker as his father, was born in 1577 and a Jane Walker, baptized 23rd May, 1579, and buried 15th October, 1609, was probably their daughter. A Joan Walker, baptized 5th September, 1574, could have been their first child, but no other entries in the West Hanningfield registers can be connected with the Architector with any reasonable probability.

His name does not appear in the court rolls covering his early manhood, but the fact that his father is occasionally referred to here as John Walker,

Senior, suggests that he was living at home or at least not far away for long enough to be forgotten. The court rolls for 1586-92 are missing and there is no mention of him in the courts for 1592-97, but his name appears frequently in the surviving rolls from 1598 to 1602, and again, from 1609 to 1625.[21] There may seem to be little value in knowing, for instance, that he acquired lands adjacent to Kents in 1597, was a member of the homage in 1598, bailiff in 1600 and again in 1612, constable in 1601, and was ordered to scour his ditch in 1625; but these entries do show that wherever he may have been in early manhood, he was never far from West Hanningfield in the last 30 years of his life. But no evidence from court rolls could ever do much to summon a man from the obscurity of past time. It is only in his surviving work that the extent of the Architector's general education, technical training and artistic skill can be seen; how they were acquired must remain, alas, an exercise in speculation.

In his notes on the Walkers, Brian Smith has made some useful and interesting speculations.[22] He points out that carpenters of the third quarter of the 16th century were much concerned with the building and rebuilding of timber-framed houses at the beginning of what was to prove one of the great rebuilding periods in English history. Then he goes on to say that 'John Walker in his early surveys calls himself architector (Tilbury) or architector and surveyor (Boxted and Hatfield Peverel), while later he almost always calls himself architector. However, it would seem that at first he drew some distinction between architector and surveyor. Normally at this time architector was a title reserved for designers of houses (*ex inf.* John Harvey in letter to Irvine Gray, 11.2.1949),[23] and *I would submit that John was actively engaged in building work.* This is something that cannot be tested, but the following circumstantial points may be recalled—his father was a carpenter and his elder brother, Cyprian, was a carpenter, and his drawings of timber-framed houses on his maps show acute and accurate observation far in advance of the crude or conventional drawings done by his contemporaries and successors.' This is quite reasonable speculation; a transition from carpenter's shop and framing yard to surveyor's drawing board is a logical one. But *how* this was achieved, *what* the training consisted of in those early days of estate surveying and mapmaking, and *who* gave this technical training, are all questions for which the answers must be based on yet more speculation.

Patronage may have helped—as it helped many an Elizabethan, including Shakespeare. However, the only hint of any evidence is an early written survey of the Hanningfields, 1592, described as being 'by John Walker, Architect, in the presence of and by the direction of Richard Cannon, gent., for the use and in the service of Edward Nevell, Lord of Bergevenny'. The Lords Bergavenny were lords of the manors which comprise the

Hanningfields and likeliest persons to be Walker's patrons. Indeed, quite apart from his technical training, it is difficult to see how he could have achieved otherwise the degree of *general* education seen in the descriptive prefaces to some of the maps and surveys (see Chronological Catalogue). There is no evidence to show if he attended any of the local grammar schools; moreover his father was illiterate, not able to sign his will.

For his technical training there are only two inconclusive scraps of evidence. His second earliest surviving survey (River Hall, Boxted, 1586) was carried out for John Ive. Boxted is close to the home of Ralph Agas at Stoke-by-Nayland, and Ive was possibly related to Agas's brother-in-law.[24] This 'link' with the only early estate mapmaker to be recorded in the *Dictionary of National Biography* is woefully tenuous; scarcely less so are the 'links' with another early mapmaker, Israel Amyce, who was living in North Essex, 1586-99, serving as a justice of the peace there and working as a surveyor.[25] One of these 'links' is a deed of the manor of Sheriffs in Colne Engaine and Earls Colne in 1604,[26] which refers back to a survey (now lost) made by 'John Walker Architecte' in 1589. Israel Amyce was closely connected with Earls Colne. This was the centre of the Essex estates of Edward de Vere, 17th Earl of Oxford, poet and courtier; and Amyce was one of the Commissioners appointed to administer those estates.[27] Moreover, in 1598, Amyce himself drew a map of Earls Colne.[28] The second 'link' occurs in the papers of Sir John Petre as principal collector in Essex for the 'Armada' Loans of 1588-89.[29] Here the entry 'Israel Amisse, arm., at Chelmissforde the XVth of March, 1588, L^{li}' is immediately followed by 'John Walker of Brundon[30] there the same daye, XXV^{li}'; this cannot be mere chance. That Walker was living at Brundon is not surprising; his work at times must have entailed living away from West Hanningfield for long periods. Moreover, he *was* working in north Essex in those years: his Boxted survey was made in 1586 and there is that missing survey of Earls Colne in 1589. Again, it should be noted that before 1586, Amyce was living at Barking and Walker's earliest surviving work is his survey of West Tilbury in 1584; and both of these places are in south Essex. There are, too, points of resemblance in both men's mapwork, although Walker's is vastly superior. Thin and inconclusive though the evidence is, it seems much more likely that Amyce, rather than Agas, was Walker's master.[31]

Very little is known about John Walker, the Architector's son. Indeed, it is only by looking closely at his maps—his achievements—that anything much can be deduced about him. In the chapter on 'Draughtsmanship and Calligraphy' the script of the two Walkers have been carefully compared, and in a number of entries in the Chronological Catalogue there has been further examinination on stylistic and palaeographical grounds. The result has been that maps which hitherto had been attributed to the Architector or to father and son jointly have now been shown conclusively to be the son's work. In quality of execution he may have been even slightly superior to his father, certainly in his lettering; but, of course, he stood on his father's shoulders, and both were consummate craftsmen.

A few facts are worth mentioning. His name appears in the West Hanningfield court roll for 1612, and again in 1618.[32] On 24th June, 1611, when he was 34, he was married at Chelmsford to Penelope Warner of South Hanningfield.[33] No children are recorded in the West Hanningfield register. He died in 1618 and was buried at West Hanningfield on 9th April; but well before this, in 1616, the last two surviving maps had been drawn. The old Architector lived on; he was buried at West Hanningfield in 8th June, 1626. The rest is silence; but a goodly part of their legacy survives.

The third mapmaker, Samuel Walker, was baptised at West Hanningfield on 19th January, 1595. His parentage is not given; it is likely, but by no means certain, that he was a son of Cyprian Walker, the carpenter, brother of the Architector (see table, p.28). Cyprian had married Margerie Hopton in 1576. At least five of the children given in the West Hanningfield baptisms, ranging from 1578-1598, are theirs—they are all beneficiaries in Cyprian's will, 1631.[34] Samuel was not a beneficiary, although he was a witness; but he (and a Margaret Walker, baptised and buried in 1596) would fit nicely into the date gaps in Cyprian's brood. Moreover, the fact that he was not a beneficiary does not prove that he was not Cyprian's child. Earlier, neither the Architector nor his brother, Richard, were beneficiaries under their father's will; maybe they did not need meagre legacies, and this may well have been true of Samuel in 1631.

He seems to have been a moderately prosperous yeoman. In 1630, William, 2nd Lord Petre, who had acquired the Hanningfield manors, granted him a lease for 21 years of Ovill's Farm and various lands, amounting to 103 acres;[35] these were of the demesnes of East Hanningfield manor and lay across the boundaries of East and West Hanningfield parishes. This lease was really a renewal: he was already in occupation of these lands and had been prior to 1627.[36] His name appears as witness in a number of leases around 1627[37] and he was bailiff of the manor in 1621 and 1630.[38] His surviving work indicates that he was a good field surveyor but the draughtsmanship of the maps is that of a fairly competent amateur; whereas John the Architector and his son were highly professional in every respect. Samuel and his wife, Ann, had three, possibly four, children. She died in 1638.[39] He was then alive, but cannot be traced after that date.* Indeed, by then most of the Walkers had left West Hanningfield or had died out. A few names appear in the last quarter of the century, but none afterwards.

*See page 17.

Notes and References

Unless stated otherwise, all catalogue numbers refer to documents in the Essex Record Office.

1. Reaney: *Place-Names of Essex* (Cambridge, 1935), 253.
2. D/DP M837.
3. D/DP M868.
4. *Royal Commission on Historical Monuments (Essex)*, IV, 167.
5. Stock and West Hanningfield, *c.* 1600 [D/DP P7]. West Hanningfield, 1611 [D/DZe 5]. East Hanningfield (with parts of West Hanningfield), 1615 [D/DP P10].
6. D/DP M838.
7. Alice was unmarried in 1514 [D/DP M839]. Her son, John Walker, the carpenter, was over 17 in 1534 [D/DP M839]. Thus, Thomas must have married Alice, *c.* 1515.
8. D/DP M839.
9. D/DP M839.
10. D/DP M839, 840.
11. D/DP M840.
12. D/DP M840.
13. D/DP M840.
14. D/DP M842.
15. D/P 247/1/1.
16. *Trans.* Essex Arch. Soc., Old Series, II, 228.
17. D/DP M844, 845.
18. D/DP M845.
19. D/ABW 40/123.
20. D/P 247/1/1.
21. D/DP M844, 845.
22. 'The Walker Family of West Hanningfield.' Typescript notes compiled February, 1965.
23. Original letter, T/G 9.
24. Irvine Gray, 'Maps of 350 years Ago', *Country Life* (16th May, 1947).
25. D/P 214/25/9; Q/SR 115/27, 118/78; D/DU 204/2, 3, 5; D/DCw T46A.
26. D/DSx 49.
27. D/DRg 2/27.
28. D/DSm P1.
29. D/DP O6/15.
30. Ballingdon-cum-Brundon was then a conjoined parish on the north Essex border. It is now part of the borough of Sudbury, Suffolk.
31. When the evidence is meagre, it is worth trying to squeeze it thoroughly. The fact that Walker paid as much as £25 in 1588/89 may

be an indication that he was well-established and doing well. Moreover, what were Amyce and Walker doing together at Chelmsford in March 1589? Amyce was of the Commission of the Peace; Sir John Petre, Collector of the loan, and his friend, Sir Thomas Mildmay, dominated the Essex Bench; almost certainly all were in Chelmsford for the Assizes. Was Amyce about to recommend Walker to Mildmay, lord of the manors of Chelmsford and Moulsham?—Walker's two great maps of Chelmsford and Moulsham were produced in 1591.

32. D/DP M845, for both years.
33. D/P 94/1/2.
34. D/ABW 50/82.
35. D/DP T182/15.
36. D/DP T77.
37. D/DP T17, T182/15, 16.
38. D/DP M845, 846.
39. D/P 247/1/1.

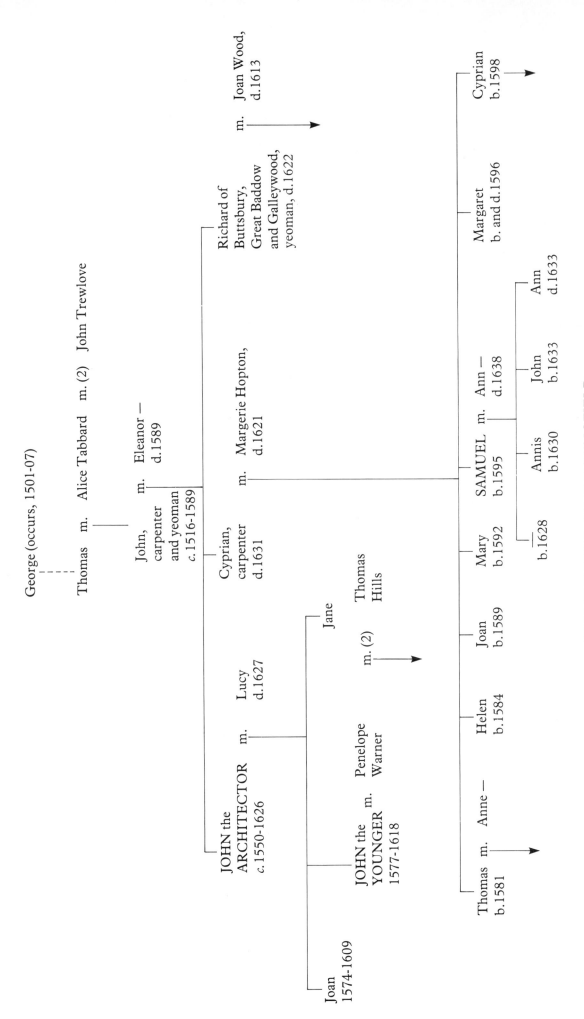

THE WALKERS OF HANNINGFIELD

The absolute accuracy of parts of this table cannot be guaranteed: Joan and Jane were *probably* the daughters of John the Architector; Samuel and his 'brothers and sisters' were all *probably* the children of Cyprian, the carpenter.

George (occurs, 1501-07)

Thomas   m.   Alice Tabbard   m. (2)   John Trewlove

John,   m.   Eleanor —
carpenter   d.1589
and yeoman
c.1516-1589

Richard of
Buttsbury,
Great Baddow
and Galleywood,
yeoman, d.1622

m. → Joan Wood, d.1613

Cyprian,   m.   Margerie Hopton,
carpenter   d.1621
d.1631

JOHN the   m.   Lucy
ARCHITECTOR   d.1627
c.1550-1626

Jane

JOHN the   m.   Penelope
YOUNGER   Warner
1577-1618

Thomas
Hills

m. (2) →

Joan
1574-1609

SAMUEL   m.   Ann —
b.1595   d.1638

Cyprian
b.1598 →

Margaret
b. and d.1596

Ann
d.1633

John
b.1633

Annis
b.1630

b.1628

Mary
b.1592

Joan
b.1589

Helen
b.1584

Thomas   m.   Anne — →
b.1581

Draughtsmanship
and
Calligraphy

In considering the 'Walker maps' as a whole, it is important continuously to bear in mind that the work of two surveyors is involved, for at first glance they all seem to be from one hand. In one sense, it might be said, this is of no great significance, for in all essentials a detailed appraisal of the work of John Walker senior holds good for that of his son.

It is, in fact, of the greatest importance to establish the identifiable differences, for upon them hinges an evaluation of the contribution of each to that not inconsiderable proportion of the extant maps (and one written survey) which bear the names of both father and son. This applies equally to the authorship of two bearing no name and another where the name or names are illegible, and, in the event, of four of these signed John Walker without further qualification.

Map or Written Survey	Name(s) of Surveyor(s) stated on map
1. West Tilbury, 1584	John Walker 'Architect"
2. Boxted, 1586	John Walker 'Architecte'
3. Hatfield Peverel, 1589	John Walker 'Architect"
4. Broomfield, 1591	John Walker
5. Chelmsford, 1591	(a) John Walker 'Architector' (map)
	(b) John Walker 'measurer' (survey)
6. Chelmsford (Moulsham), 1591	John Walker 'Architector'
7. East, West & South Hanningfield, 1592	John Walker 'Architect'
8. Terling, 1597	John Walker 'Architector'
9. West & East Horndon, etc., 1598	John Walker
10. Chignall (Writtle), 1599	John Walker
11. Purleigh, 1600	John Walker
12. Danbury, Purleigh, c. 1600	John Walker
13. Stock & West Hanningfield, c. 1600	[Not stated]
14. West Hanningfield, 1601	[Illegible]
15. Ingatestone, 1600-01	John Walker the elder and John Walker the younger
16. Ingatestone, 1602	[Not stated]
17. Ingatestone & Mountnessing, 1605	John Walker senior and John Walker junior
18. Matching, 1609	John Walker senior and John Walker junior
19. White Roothing, 1609	John Walker junior
20. Little Leighs, 1609	John Walker senior and John Walker junior
21. Mundon, 1612	John Walker senior and John Walker junior
22. Andover (Hants.), 1614	John Walker junior
23. East, West & South Hanningfield, 1614	John Walker senior and John Walker junior
24. East Hanningfield, 1615	John Walker senior and John Walker junior
25. South Hanningfield, c. 1615	[Not stated]
26. Stock & Buttsbury, 1616	John Walker
27. Tolleshunt D'Arcy & Tolleshunt Major, 1616	John Walker
28. Springfield, c. 1616	John Walker senior and John Walker junior

One must, therefore, first compare those maps which are undoubtedly the sole work of the elder Walker (Nos. 1, 2, 5, 6, 8 above), all bearing the name John Walker with the distinction 'Architect' or 'Architector', with those (Nos. 19 and 22) which are signed by John Walker junior alone. To those ascribable to the older man may be added one further map (No. 4), for in 1591 his son was still in his early teens.

Representation of Features

A close comparison of their respective methods of representing features yields distinguishing marks only with difficulty. There is a tendency for the older man to use denser colours, particularly the green with which meadows, pastures and greens are infilled (compare, for example, Plate V and Plate XIX); his thatched roofs are mostly a brownish colour, while on his son's two maps they are light yellow (compare, for example, Plate I and Plate XXI), otherwise their representations of buildings are identical; hedges and trees are very similarly treated by both, but there is sometimes a difference in their respective delineations of fences (compare, for example, Plate XII and Plate XVIII(b)). These few distinctions and the sense of an overall lighter touch in the younger man's draughtsmanship apart, the representational work of John Walker junior is virtually a 'carbon copy' of his father's.

The Scripts

It is to the scripts employed by the two men that one must turn for the aspect that most distinguishes the maps of the one from those of the other.

John Walker senior had at his command a number of scripts, each serving a different role on his maps. For his main titles he normally used an undistinguished derivation of the formal text hand (Figs. 1, 2) and for the descriptive tables a bastard secretary hand adulterated with Roman in the case of certain capital letters (Figs. 3, 4).

(Fig. 1)
From Chelmsford (Moulsham), 1591

(Fig. 2)
From Terling, 1597

(Fig. 3)
From Terling, 1597

(Fig. 4)
From Terling, 1597

Occasionally the formal text hand, rather better done, may be used for principal place-names on the body of the map (Fig. 5) and frequently for the points of the compass; sparingly Roman capitals fulfil the same purpose (Fig. 6).

The new parke.   THE . OVLDE . PARKE .

(Fig. 5)   (Fig. 6)
From West Horndon, 1598   From West Horndon, 1598

For field and other place-names lettering which is a curious mixture of Roman and Italic is almost invariably found (Figs. 7-9).

Bexfells lande   Maddikes grene ·   Greate Wyndmill fielde

(Fig. 7)   (Fig. 8)   (Fig. 9)
Moulsham, 1591   Terling, 1597   Terling, 1597

John Walker junior too was master of a number of hands. On the evidence of the two maps which bear his name alone he employed for his titles and other main headings a formal text hand worthy of any writing-master of the period (Fig. 10). This hand introduced the main descriptive 'Table' which was then continued in an equally fine, if less elaborate, mixed formal text and bastard secretary or engrossing script (Fig. 11).

Malcalls Bury .   A Trewe and perfect platt
                          landes belongeinge or apperteyninge to t

(Fig. 10)   (Fig. 11)
White Roothing, 1609   White Roothing, 1609

In strong contrast to these hands field and most other place-names are entered on the maps in a graceful Italic (Figs. 12-14).

Matchinge Greene   Bury Crofte .   Mill Fielde .

(Fig. 12)   (Fig. 13)   (Fig. 14)
White Roothing, 1609   White Roothing, 1609   White Roothing, 1609

Italic is also used for the other 'Tables' (Fig. 15) and to record other information, sometimes mixed with a secretary hand (Fig. 16).

(Fig. 15)
White Roothing, 1609

(Fig. 16)
White Roothing, 1609

For sub-headings and sparingly for some important place-names John junior employed a round, upright hand with long ascenders which are slightly barbed at the top (Fig. 17). Inherently less attractive than the other scripts, it is the one that he handles least well.

(Fig. 17)
White Roothing, 1609

A close examination thus demonstrates that however closely John junior copied his father in draughtsmanship, he did not slavishly imitate him in lettering his maps, but clearly took as his models examples in contemporary writing manuals. It is in this aspect above all that the younger man must be rated significantly his father's superior.

But as has been hinted above, a study of their relative capabilities as calligraphers and draughtsmen has an importance greater than a mere assessment of which was the better mapmaker, for related to a lighter overall treatment it proves conclusively that John Walker junior was the draughtsman of *all* surviving maps bearing the names of both father and son (Nos. 15, 17, 18, 24, 28 in the above list).

Of the six maps, bearing the name John Walker without qualification, in which both men might have had a hand, that of 1598 (No. 9) is doubtless by the older man; those of 1600 and *c.*1600 (Nos. 11, 12) are examples of joint work; that of 1599 (No. 10) is almost entirely by John junior, and the two dated 1616 (Nos. 26, 27) are wholly his work. The unsigned map of *c.*1600 (No. 13) is by John senior, while that of 1601 (No. 14) on which the name or names are illegible is truly a joint work. The other unsigned map dated to *c.*1615 (No. 25) is by neither father nor son and is considered to be by Samuel Walker. By the criteria of handwriting, the written surveys of 1589, 1591 and 1592 (Nos. 3, 5(b), 7) are each the work of an unknown scribe, and that of 1602 (No. 16) is explicitly so and may have been a copy of a survey made by the Walkers to accompany the map of 1600-01 (No. 15), or it may have been compiled by the scribe from details in the map itself. The survey of 1614 (No. 20), although bearing the names of both men, was written by John junior.*

The list of their extant works given above may now be augmented thus:—

Map or Survey	Field-Surveyor(s)	Draughtsman and/or Scribe
1. West Tilbury, 1584	John Walker 'Architect''	John Walker senior
2. Boxted, 1586	John Walker 'Architecte'	John Walker senior
3. Hatfield Peverel, 1589	John Walker 'Architect''	An unnamed scribe
4. Broomfield, 1591	John Walker	John Walker senior
5. Chelmsford, 1591	(a) John Walker 'Architector' (map)	John Walker senior
	(b) John Walker 'measurer' (survey)	An unnamed scribe
6. Chelmsford (Moulsham), 1591	John Walker Architector	John Walker senior
7. East, West & South Hanningfield, 1592	John Walker 'Architect'	An unnamed scribe
8. Terling, 1597	John Walker 'Architector'	John Walker senior
9. West & East Horndon, etc., 1598	John Walker	John Walker senior
10. Chignall (Writtle), 1599	John Walker	John Walker senior and junior
11. Purleigh, 1600	John Walker	John Walker senior and junior
12. Danbury, Purleigh, etc., c.1600	John Walker	John Walker senior and junior
13. Stock & West Hanningfield, c.1600	[Not given]	John Walker senior
14. West Hanningfield, 1601	[Illegible]	John Walker senior and junior
15. Ingatestone, 1600-01	John Walker the elder and John Walker the younger	John Walker junior
16. Ingatestone, 1602	[Not given]	An unnamed scribe
17. Ingatestone & Mountnessing, 1605	John Walker senior and junior	John Walker junior
18. Matching, 1609	John Walker senior and junior	John Walker junior
19. White Roothing, 1609	John Walker junior	John Walker junior
20. Little Leighs, 1609	John Walker senior and junior	John Walker junior
21. Mundon, 1612	John Walker senior and junior	John Walker junior
22. Andover (Hants.), 1614	John Walker junior	John Walker junior
23. East, West & South Hanningfield, 1614	John Walker senior and junior	John Walker junior
24. East Hanningfield, 1615	John Walker senior and junior	John Walker junior
25. South Hanningfield, c.1615	[Not given]	Samuel Walker
26. Stock & Buttsbury, 1616	John Walker	John Walker junior
27. Tolleshunt D'Arcy and Major, 1616	John Walker	John Walker junior
28. Springfield, c.1616	John Walker senior and junior	John Walker junior

*For a more detailed appraisal of all these maps and surveys, see the individual entries in the Chronological Catalogue and accompanying Plates.

Interpreting the evidence offered by the list, it would seem that however long before he may have aided his father, as his apprentice in field-surveying, it was not until 1599, at the age of 21 or 22, that John junior was allowed to participate in the draughtsmanship of the final version of a map and then without acknowledgement (No. 10), suggesting that his years of training were long and rigorous. In the next year, however, his name, coupled with his father's, appears for the first time on a map (No. 15) and rightly so, for in its finished state it is entirely his work. And excepting the map of West Hanningfield, 1601 (No. 14) and that of South Hanningfield, c. 1615 (No. 25), so it was to be thereafter.

Although the eventual discovery of further maps might alter the attributions somewhat, the fact that there is no map by the hand of John Walker senior between 1601 and the year of his death (1626), suggests that for some unknown physical cause he found draughtsmanship and calligraphy difficult and even impossible throughout that period. His legs and his spirit allowed him to participate still in the field-survey work, hence the appearance of his name on the 'joint' maps, until the death of his son in 1618. But that unhappy event probably brought about his complete retirement after over thirty years spent in his craft. This may have occurred even before John junior's death, for on the two maps of 1616 (Nos. 26 and 27) he felt it unnecessary for the first time to qualify his name with 'junior'. It is likely that 1616 saw a rapid falling-off of John junior's ability for the last three maps (Nos. 26-28) display a remarkable lapse from the standards of grace and taste shown in all his other work. Illness on his part and the inability of his father may well explain why the map of South Hanningfield (No.25) was drawn by Samuel Walker.*

In the first 'Table or Index' to his fine map of the Manor of Foxcott in Hampshire (No. 22), John Walker junior began, 'Forasmuch as it is a thinge usuall amongst manie Surveyours, and also in my Judgement most necessarie & needefull first to sett down some direcc[i]ons to be as it were a Lanthorne and light for the Lord or Owner of the landes of which any Survey is made . . .' These words epitomise the wholly professional attitude and dedication of both father and son to their craft. Just as their maps and surveys must have indeed been like lanthorns and lights revealing so much about their estates to those landowners who had the good sense to commission them, so today they continue to illuminate with an undiminished, unique brilliance our understanding of the landscape and buildings, tenure and custom of a significant part of Essex in the decades about the turn of the 16th century.

*For a consideration of Samuel Walker's draughtsmanship and calligraphy, see the comments on his maps in the Chronological Catalogue.

A
Chronological
Catalogue

EXPLANATORY NOTES ON THE CATALOGUE

FORM OF ENTRY

Heading (in capitals): Gives name(s) of parish(es) concerned and date of map.

References: In square brackets on same line as heading.

Size, media and condition: Size is expressed in centimetres correct to the nearest millimetre and in inches correct to the nearest $\frac{1}{16}$th inch. Whether a map is on parchment or paper is stated; its physical condition is described. As almost all the maps are ink and watercolour (only one being drawn simply in ink) and each is illustrated, it is felt unnecessary to repeat this information in each entry.

Title: Copied literally from map.

Surveyor(s): Copied literally from map.

Scale: As stated on map; expressed also (in round brackets) in inches to the mile. If the original has no scale it has been calculated in chains to the inch and inches to the mile.

Area surveyed: Where possible the acreage stated on the map is given, otherwise it is calculated. The parts of a parish covered are given, e.g. 'N., NE. and S. of parish'. In the case of written surveys, their contents are summarised.

Commissioned by: The name of the person at whose behest the survey was carried out is transcribed from the map where stated; otherwise it is given in square brackets, if ascertainable.

Comment: As both individually and jointly John Walker senior and John Walker junior show great uniformity in their treatment of natural and man-made features and as the essential parts of their maps and those of Samuel Walker and Andrew Pease are individually illustrated, it is felt unnecessary to describe in each entry the way in which the features are represented. Where there is some aspect of particular note or a departure from normal practice, attention is drawn to it. Otherwise the *Comment* is concerned to underline the development of the craft of the surveyors, to evaluate the quality of each map or written survey and, in the case of those bearing the names of both John Walker senior and John Walker junior, to establish whether father, son or both were responsible for the draughtsmanship.

1.—WEST TILBURY, 1584   [E.R.O., D/DU 23/138]

Volume, 30.2×20.3cm. (11$\frac{7}{8}$×8in.), paper (watermark uniform throughout), parchment covers (original, inscribed on front with title in red ink (in surveyor's hand)), 42 pages including blanks. Condition: good.

Title
The Suruey of West tilbury A[nn]o 1584 vltimo die augusti.

Surveyor
John Walker Architect'.

Scale
Given only in a note at end of volume [see *Summary of Contents* (iii)]: 32 rods to euery yntch (10in. to 1m.).

Summary of Contents
(i)   *Written* and *mapped* survey of demesne lands [192 acres] of the Manor of West Tilbury, excluding marshes· and commons. Written descriptions on *verso,* map on facing *recto* side of page, keyed to each other by reference letters; 8 maps of separate parcels of land drawn on every other opening (pp.2-31).
(ii) *Written* survey only, being 'A Contente of all the marsh grwndes (*sic*) And co[m]mons Aswell fresh as Saltens belonging to the man[n]or of West tilbury . . .' [615 acres] (pp.32-41).
(iii) On p.42: 'Behowlde this platt Following (*sic*) whose Scale is Alowed 32 rods to euery yntch . . . lause deo Amen' [in the surveyor's hand].

Commissioned by
[Andrew Jenour of Bigods in Great Dunmow.]

Comment
This earliest surviving example of the work of John Walker senior contains much that is characteristic of his later maps: the accuracy of the surveying, given the standards and equipment of the day, the close attention to detail in representing both natural and artificial features; but there is a certain lack of finish, perhaps denoting relative inexperience, and the sparse use of rather drab, impure colours is not 'typical', notably in the representation of field-boundaries. It is to the careful delineation of buildings in elevation that the eye is immediately drawn (see Plate I which reproduces all

buildings except a post-mill and three tiny outbuildings shown with thatched roofs and exposed timbers). The evidence on several of the maps that a good deal of the land lay in strips (some consolidated) in common fields is of particular interest.

2.—BOXTED, 1586   [E.R.O., D/DEl P1]

Volume, 34.6×22.2cm. (13⅝×8¾in.), paper (watermark uniform throughout), parchment covers (original, repaired, modern end papers) with embossed scrollwork device in a frame, all in gold (rubbed), on front and back, with 'Com' Essex: Riuers Hall Nº 1' written on front in contemporary or near contemporary hand, 104 pages including title page and blanks. Condition: good.

Title
A Suruey of Riuers Hall in Boxsted in the County of Essex this laste of Aprill 1586.

Surveyor
John Walker Architecte.

Scale
No scale or scale bar given [5ch. to 1in. (16in. to 1m.)].

Summary of Contents
(i)   *Written* description of 'Demeines to riuers Hall' [517 acres] (pp.1-19). At end, signature of 'John Walker'.
(ii) Detailed introductory note on tenure, customs, etc., to written and mapped survey of 'Customary landes' (pp.22-23).
(iii) *Written* and *mapped* survey of 'Customary landes' [458 acres]. Written description on *verso*, map on facing *recto* side of page, keyed to each other by reference letters; 14 maps of individual customary estates.

Commissioned by
John Ive.

Comment
The passage of two years since the survey of West Tilbury Hall demesnes

had brought noteworthy development in Walker's approach to his craft. It is not merely in the visually obvious aspects, as a use of colour more nearly that employed in all his later work or the more professional finish to the maps, that this is apparent (see Plate III); it is also that for the first time something of his own personality comes through in the written part of the survey. The West Tilbury survey is a competent but—despite his name being upon it—anonymous piece of work, detailed, even painstaking, but offering nothing by way of comment or advice to anyone using it.

Walker's commission at Boxted was to survey both the demesne and the customary lands of the manor. This time he elected to provide a written description of the demesne but to map and to describe in words the tenants' holdings. As in the West Tilbury volume, he began by setting this down without preamble. In three columns each constituent field or other parcel of the demesne is described as to its individual land-use, its abuttal with an adjacent field, its name, acreage and annual leasehold value (unless woodland, in which case a note on the standing timber is usually substituted). Before embarking upon the plotting and description of the tenants' lands, however, Walker provides a two-page introduction which he heads lengthily but instructively:

> A trew Suruey taken and p[ar]ticuler plattes Made of all the Customary landes and tenementes as also all and Severall the woodes/howlden of Rivers hawlle in Boxsted in the County of Essex the laste of Aprill in the xxviij[th] yeare of the reygne of our Soveragne lady qvene Elizabeth by the grace of god [et]c' for the worshipfull John Ive Essqvyer. and Secondary of her magestyes Crowne office/by John Walker architect' and Surveyer by the assistaunce and ayde of William Sickerlinge. Robert Shinglewood. John Shinglewood. John Fysher Edwarde messinge/Rycharde Downes Beniamine Cleare Steven Chillan Allin Sunday w[i]*th* divers others Customary Tenantes to the seid mano[u]*r* whose Customes are as followeth.

There follows a succinct account of the general customs attaching to the copyhold lands or, as Walker expresses it, 'An thus in a shorte Sum I have Shewed the moste speciall Customes of the Coppyhowlde landes and tenementes . . .' He then completes the Introduction with 'A note for the Reader as followeth Concerning the order for the fynding oute of any thing herin that you desyer to know', being explicit instructions on how to use the maps and written description. Such helpful explanatory notes, often in yet greater detail, are to become a hallmark of Walker's later maps and surveys.

It is also possible for the first time to test Walker's accuracy in representing buildings, including minor detail, against a surviving monument that has important features substantially the same as in his day—Boxted church, although it was much altered in the 17th and 18th centuries. It would appear that he drew the elevation of the south front of the church on an enlarged horizontal scale of 2 chains to 1 inch, which gives the following base lengths: chancel, 20ft. $7\frac{1}{2}$in.; south aisle/nave, 41ft. 3in.; tower, 18ft. $6\frac{3}{4}$in. According to the plan in *R.C.H.M.*, Essex, iii, 9, the true measurements are 24ft., 45ft. and 15ft. respectively. Given the smallness of the scale the margins of error are not great. The chancel today has the remains of an early 16th-century gable cross at its E. end: Walker shows this complete and another at the E. end of the nave (which disappeared when the thatched roof of Walker's day was rebuilt less steeply pitched). He also shows correctly that the tower is of four stages, that its embattled brick parapet on the S. side has four *merlons,* that its S. wall has a single-light window in the second stage (a similar window is also shown in the third stage, but this, no doubt, disappeared when the wall 'was rebuilt in the 16th century' [*R.C.H.M.*]), and that it is buttressed, as is the E. wall of the chancel. For a discussion of certain secular buildings, see pp.87-8; for an analysis of all buildings, see Table 1 (p.97) also Plates III and XXXVIII.

3.—HATFIELD PEVEREL, 1589   [E.R.O., D/DBd M6/2]

Volume, 27.9×19.7cm. (11×7$\frac{3}{4}$in.), paper (watermark uniform throughout), thread sewn but unbound, 10 folios, including blanks. Condition: good.

Title
A trew Survey. and contents of the Mano[u]r of Mugden Hall w[i]*th* all the demeyn lands, meadowes & woods thereunto belonginge. as also all the customarie lands w[i]*th* there p[ro]fitts & contents, and all the free holde rent[es] and services as they now are scituate in the paroches & feilds of Hatfeild Gultinge [Ulting] Borham, Terlinge, & little Baddow in the Countie of Essex, survehed the X[th] of November in the yere of our Lorde god. 1589. & in xxxj[th] yere of Queene Elizabeth &c'. by John Walker Architect' & Surveyor. And this Mannor hath both courte, and lete, and charter warrant.

Surveyor
See *Title.*

Summary of Contents
(i) demesne (ff. 1-4); (ii) copyholds (f. 5); freeholds (ff. 5-6). [See Plate IV for specimen entries indicative of the degree of detail.] There are no maps.

Commissioned by
[John Aylmer, Bishop of London.]

Comment
Although in a contemporary hand, this copy of the written survey was not penned by John Walker senior. The layout in three columns is similar to that in the survey of Boxted, 1586, and it is likely therefore to be a rather hurriedly written copy of one in Walker's hand, now lost. There is also an early 17th-century copy (E.R.O., D/DBd M6/1) in which the order of contents is (i) copyholds; (ii) freeholds; and (iii) demesne.

4.—BROOMFIELD, 1591   [E.R.O., D/DVk1]

28.3×33.2cm. ($11\frac{1}{8} \times 13\frac{1}{16}$in.), parchment (single skin). Condition: good.

Title
Widdow wealdes land and Tenement Called Tylers Walls and Wakemans.

Surveyor
John Walker.

Scale
No scale or scale bar given [4ch. to 1in. (20in. to 1m.)].

Area mapped
41 acres is SE. of parish on E. side of Chelmsford road.

Commissioned by
[Unknown]

Comment
Although the map is of only a small farm, Walker bestows the same care in delineation, lettering and use of colour as in his other more major works, as may be seen in the portion reproduced as Plate IV.

5.—CHELMSFORD, 1591   [E.R.O., D/DM P1; D/DGe M50]

(i)   *Map.* 71.4×74.9cm. (28⅛×29½in.), parchment (single skin).
(ii) *Written Survey.* Volume, 42.2×27.9cm. (16⅝×11in.), paper (watermark uniform throughout), board covers bound in leather, blind tooled with the words 'BISHOPS HALL' on front; 45 folios, including blanks. Condition: good.

Title
(i)   *Map.* A Trew Plat of the man[n]or And towne of chellmisforde. 1591.
(ii) *Written Survey.* The Manor of chelmersforde A booke of the Survey and admeasurem[en]*t* of the saide Mano[u]*r*, demeasnes & s[e]rvic[es], lib[er]ties Franchesies & other hereditam[en]*t[es]* of the saide Mano[u]*r* by exact views of the same, vppon the searche of the Courte rolls, rentalls, and other materiall escriptes of the said Mano[u]r, at the Courte Leete, & Courte Baron there holden for the righte worshipfull' S[i]*r* Thomas Mildemaye knighte, on Twesdaye the twentith daye of June in the three and thirtith yere of the reigne of o[u]*r* Sou[er]eigne Lady Quene Elizabeth before Edward Moryson Esquire S[ur]veyo[u]*r* John Lathum gent' Steward, & John Walker measurer, Rob[er]te wood and other ten*a*nt[es] and suito[u]*r*s there.

Surveyor
(i)   *Map.* John Walker Architector.
(ii) *Written Survey.* See *Title.*

Scale
Scale bar of 6in. to 96p. (20in. to 1m.).

Area mapped
598 acres (excluding 'backsydes', gardens and orchards in the town) in centre and N. of parish.

Summary of Contents of Written Survey
(i)   'Of the Manor of Chelmersford' [A general description of the manor and town. See Plate VI] (f.2).
(ii)   'Of the Scyte and demeasne Landes of the saide Mano[u]*r*' (299 acres) (ff.3-5).
(iii) 'Of certayne Quillett[es]' [i.e. small unenclosed plots of land, in this case part of the demesne used for the sites of the tollhouse or court house, fair and market, market cross, and four tenements held by the church (two for the relief of the poor)] (f.6).

(iv) 'Of the freholde Tenem[en]t[es] & their Tennant[es] on the west side of the saide towne of Chelmesford' (ff.7-10).

(v) 'Of the Freholde Ten[emen]t[es] & their Tennant[es] on the Easte side of the said towne' (ff.11-15).

(vi) 'de lib[er]is Ten[emen]tis In Newstreete' (f.16).

(vii) 'Nowe agaynste the churchyearde' (f.17).

(viii) 'Of the freholde Ten[emen]t[es] and their Tennaunt[es] in Churchestreete al[ia]s Brockhole Lane' (ff.18-19).

(ix) 'Of the Tenem[en]t[es] In the Middle Rowe in Chelmesford and ther Tennant[es]' (ff.20-21).

(x) 'Of the Freholde Ten[emen]t[es] and their Tennant[es] being vpland' (ff.22-24).

(xi) 'Of the custom[ar]ye Ten[emen]t[es] of the vplande' (ff.25-28).

(xii) 'Of the custom[ar]ye Tenem[en]t[es] w[i]thin the towne' (ff.29-36).

(xiii) 'Of the parsonage of Chelmesford' (f.38).

(xiv) 'Of the lib[er]tyes and franchesyes of the aforesaide Mano[u]r of Chelmesford' (f.39).

(xv) 'Of customes and seruices of the manor aforesaid' (ff.40-41).

(xvi) Summary valuation of the manor and totals of freeholders and copyholders (158) and of freehold and customary tenements (209) (f.42).

(xvii) 'Rentes decayed & other services' [one entry only] (f.44).

Commissioned by
Sir Thomas Mildmay.

Comment
The survival of the Chelmsford map of 1591 allows us to see how John Walker's craftsmanship, of which the West Tilbury and Boxted surveys give so much promise, reached its perfection. The mapping of Chelmsford town and its hamlet Moulsham* (see 6. below) was not only ambitious in this concept but unsurpassed in its achievement.

While there is no doubt that the map is solely by Walker—this is both explicit and implicit from the internal evidence—the written survey presents problems. The copy of the survey that has come down to us is not in Walker's hand, though the paper and writing are contemporary.** It is to be noted that although Walker in his explanatory table on the map states

---

*Moulsham is a hamlet of the parish of Chelmsford.
**The Secretary hand used is similar to, but not the same as, that used for engrossing some of the court rolls of the Manor of Chelmsford of this period [D/DM 7].

'whatsoever else you desyer to se you shalbe Satysfyed in the booke of Survey' there is no direct keying of the map to the survey. The general introduction to the survey is much in Walker's style, however, and it remains possible that we have a duplicate copied by another hand. It is also possible that it is the work of Edward Moryson described as 'Surveyour' in the title.*

It is impossible to give an accurate count of buildings in the S.E. quarter of the map which covers most of the town area. In the introduction to the written survey it is said that there were 'more than three hundred habitations', but the number of structural unities was undoubtedly fewer. The body of the survey lists 118 tenements in Chelmsford town proper, i.e., north of the river Can. A count of street-facing entrances (cartways and doorways) in the town area of the map comes to 156. These disparate figures are of little significance in themselves. The overall importance of the visual evidence may, however, be gauged in the reproduction (Plate V). On the 'upland' (rural) part of the map the buildings represented in Table 2 (p.98) do not appear in Plate V.

6.—CHELMSFORD (MOULSHAM), 1591   [E.R.O., D/DM P2]

174×82.5cm. (68½×32½in.), parchment (three conjoined skins of unequal area). Condition: good.

Title
A Trew Platt of the man[n]or and hamlett of moulsham. 1591.

Surveyor
John Walker Architector.

Scale
Scale bar of 6in. to 96p. (20in. to 1m.).

Area mapped
1,706 acres in S. of parish.

*Nothing is known of Moryson: none of his work is represented in the collections of the Essex Record Office, nor does his name appear in Peter Eden (ed.) *Dictionary of Surveyors,* 1975-6.

Commissioned by
Sir Thomas Mildmay.

Comment
On the quality of craftsmanship in this map, it is necessary only to echo the verdict offered upon that of Chelmsford town.* In the case of this map too it is impossible to give an accurate count of buildings in that part where the town spills over into the Manor of Moulsham. This area is reproduced as Plate VI; all other buildings are analysed in Table 3 (p.99). That this map was also accompanied by a written survey is borne out at the end of Walker's elaborate note to 'Right worshipful and Christian readers'. Indeed, it may have been in existence as late as 1866.**

7.—EAST, WEST AND SOUTH HANNINGFIELD, 1592 [E.R.O., D/DP M889]

44.8×30.5cm. (17⅝×12in.), parchment (one mem. written on one side only). Condition: good.

Title
Essex. A Survey and generall content[es] of all the demeine landes Earable and pasture as allsoe all woodes and meadowes belonging to the Mannor of East west hannigfielde [*sic*] and allso to the Manno[u]r of Southhany[n]fielde Scituate in the Countie of Essex surveyed and measured this Moneth of Aprill in A[nn]o do[min]i 1592. by John Walker Architect in the presence and by the direction of Richard Cannon gent' Thomas Wardoll Bayliffe of the same Lo[rdshi]*pp* with divers other Customary tenaunt[es] at the appointm[en]*t* of the saide Bayliffe for the use, and in the service of the right ho[noura]*ble* Edward Nevill Lorde of Bergevenny measured every p[ar]cell perticulerly and severally as in a grose plat is to be seene, and shall also appeare in a booke of Survey to be made out of the same platt w[i]*th* the true buttoll[es] and Content[es] of every p[ar]cell as soone as tyme will p[er]mitt.

*The Chelmsford town map also shows part of the built-up area of Moulsham south of the river Can and there are discrepancies between the two maps in the delineation of the buildings. It would appear that Walker, intending to survey Moulsham separately, was for once less than careful.
**See D. W. Coller, *The People's History of Essex*, 210. See also p.94, no.11.

A CHRONOLOGICAL CATALOGUE

Surveyor
See *Title.*

Summary of Contents
(i)   Manor of East West Hanningfield: demesne (774 acres, including park (275 acres)).
(ii) Manor of South Hanningfield: demesne (385 acres).
(iii) Farm called Blythhedges in West Hanningfield (164 acres).

Commissioned by
See *Title.*

Comment
The clear implication in the lengthy title, that Walker was only making a survey in summary form because he had already prepared a draft map and was willing to prepare 'a booke of survey . . . as soone as tyme will permitt', is underlined by his note at the end of the document: 'I haue not right ho[noura]*ble* but made a briefe note because I haue referred the butting and boundinge of every p[ar]ticuler and seuerall Close of land wood[es] and Meadowe vnto the fielde book of Survey to be made w[i]*th* a generall platt if yo[u]*r* Lo[rdshi]*p* will haue one made. Yo[u]*r* Lo[rdshi]*ps* moste humble to Commaund.' It would seem therefore that a map and detailed written survey of these manors of this date are now lost unless time did not permit until 1614-15 (see Nos. 20-22), when the task was passed to Walker's son, which seems unlikely, in view of the passage of time!

Despite the use of the first person singular this brief survey is not in Walker's hand, although contemporary (see Plate IX).

8.—TERLING, 1597   [Private Custody]

116.2×143.5cm. (45¾×56½in.), parchment (two conjoined skins of unequal area). Condition: good apart from minor tears (now repaired) and evidence of the effect of damp storage and of abrasion from unrolling and re-rolling in the past. There has been some fading, particularly affecting the heavy green colour used for meadows and pastures, indicating, probably, that the map was hung on a wall for a long period.

Title
The Mannor of Terlinge.

Surveyor
John Walker Architector.

Scale
Scale bar of 6in. to 96p. (20in. to 1m.).

Area mapped
1,274 acres, being the greater part of Terling with areas in S. and SE. of Fairstead and NW. of Hatfield Peverel.

Commissioned by
Sir John Tyrrell.

Comment
The value of a Walker survey is nowhere better demonstrated than in this map, the draughtsmanship of which may be said to meet John Walker senior's own self-imposed standards. In the 18th century the face of the village with the adjoining parkland and gardens was radically altered when the main part of the present mansion of Terling Place was built and the map is the only reliable record of their earlier layout (see Plate IX). The types of building outside the village area (i.e. not reproduced in Plate IX) are analysed in Table 4 (p.100).

9.—WEST AND EAST HORNDON,   [E.R.O., D/DP P5]
DUNTON AND BULPHAN, 1598

173.4×114.9cm. ($68\frac{1}{4}$×$45\frac{1}{4}$in.), parchment (four conjoined skins of unequal area), with separate plan of Noke Hall, 30.5×39cm. (12×$15\frac{3}{8}$in.), parchment. Condition: the top of the main map has a number of small holes (now filled by parchment repair) and is considerably faded and rubbed as a result of being the outer layer of a roll; there has been some shelling (now arrested) and fading where the skins of parchment are joined together; otherwise the condition of both maps is good.

Title
A True platt and survey of the mannors of Weast Hornedon, East Hornedon, felde house, noke hall, Ames, with the ferme called Sallmons, Belsers hatch, goate house and others: 1598.

Surveyor
John Walker.

Scale
Scale bar of 6in. to 96p. (20in. to 1m.).

Area mapped
2,585 acres, comprising almost whole of West Horndon, whole of East Horndon except N. and NE., W. of Dunton, and a small area adjacent in Ingrave and Childerditch (the larger map); and 127 acres in NE. of Bulphan (the smaller map).

Commissioned by
Sir John Petre.

Comment
In this map the elder Walker maintains his superb attention to accurate detail and nowhere better than in his representation of buildings, particularly Old Thorndon Hall with its complex elevation and extensive range of outbuildings (Plate X). This aspect of the map is fully discussed on pp.82-4 and all buildings are analysed in Table 5 (pp.101-2).

   In 'The Table or Indix For the better understandinge of this present platt and the perticulers thereof' he gives full directions for the use of the map and again in so doing reveals to us his extraordinary dedication to his profession. As on the map of the Manor of Terling, he utilises what would otherwise be blank areas of parchment to provide a table of tenants and their annual rents.

10.—CHIGNALL (WRITTLE), 1599   [E.R.O., D/DP P6]

43.2×58.7cm. (17×23⅛in.), paper. Condition: good, except for wear along folds (now flattened and strengthened).

Title
A true platt of Beamond oates* in the parish of Writtle.

Surveyor
Measured and taken the laste of November 1599 for the right worshipfull Sir John Petre knight by John Walker.

---

*A letter 'm' has been inserted with a caret mark before 'oates' at a later date, a corruption of the name occasionally found in documents, including the map (see Plate XII for the likely reason).

Scale
No scale or scale bar given [4ch. to 1in. (20in. to 1m.)].

Area mapped
241 acres, being the greater part of the former detached part 'no. 3' of the parish of Writtle now incorporated in the modern parish of Chignall.

Commissioned by
[See *Surveyor*.]

Comment
The map (see Plates XI and XII) has characteristic Walker accuracy and careful attention to buildings, but the overall lack of finish (field-boundaries represented only by a line) and an insertion in the brief written description suggest that it may have first been conceived as a draft. This is borne out too by the dry scoring of the paper to mark the boundaries before inking in (seen most clearly where unenclosed boundaries are represented by dots) and by the dots made where the boundary courses change. The showing of trees in woodland and, above all, the presence of the map in the Petre archives perhaps indicate that Sir John Petre may have been satisfied with the draft as a practical record of the farm and a more finished version was never completed.

The map has a much greater importance than is at first obvious, for closer examination reveals that although only the name John Walker, without qualification, appears upon it, it provides our first knowledge of John Walker junior as a land surveyor and mapmaker. It is unknown to what extent he was involved in the field-work, nor can it be shown that his hand delineated the field boundaries, but the use of a light, bright yellow to represent thatch rather than the brownish colour normally found on his father's maps is more in keeping with those later ones undoubtedly by the son. What is certain is that almost all the lettering is by the younger man. This is not immediately apparent from the field-names, for they are in round characters with long upright ascenders hooked at their tops, which he subsequently used sparingly for some principal place-names (see p. 34, Fig. 17, and *cf.* Plates XI and XII). Among the mixed hands used for the brief written description on the right-hand side of the map and in the hand used for notes on the plan itself there is immediately recognizable the Italic employed by John Walker junior in his maps of White Roothing, 1609, and Andover, 1614 (Plates XX and XXII). This may be seen on Plate XII in the words 'These two croftes are Gregorie Shettlewoods freeholde', noting particularly the characteristic forms of letter 'g' and the ligature 'ft'. The hand of John Walker senior is not, however entirely absent, for the title and

the four points of the compass are in his better formal text script and he
added one field-name 'moulles Crofte' (Plate XII). Compare is 'ft' ligature
with that of his son.

Plates XI, XII shows all buildings represented on the map.

11.—PURLEIGH, 1600   [E.R.O., Acc.6395: D/DHn]

76.7×57.9cm. ($30\frac{5}{16}$ × $22\frac{7}{8}$ in.), parchment. Condition: good.

Title
The demeynes of The Mannor of Waltons in Purley.

Surveyor
Surveyed measured and taken the xxviith of November in anno domini 1600
by John Walker.

Scale
No scale or scale bar given [about 4ch. to 1in. (20in. to 1m.)].

Area mapped
336 acres in W. of parish.

Commissioned by
Thomas Mildmay.

Comment
The production of this map seems almost certain to have been linked with
that of the map of Jackletts (No. 12), another Mildmay property close by.
This view was shared by the author of the endorsement to that map (see the
entry below). Certainly the maps descended in common ownership at least
until the latter half of the 18th century, for the same hands which have
added amendments during that century to the map of Jackletts have here
indicated subsequent changes to field boundaries and wooded areas. Still
more pencil additions have been made at a later date.

Like the map of Jackletts and that of Ingatestone of similar date it
appears, at least in its lettering, to be almost completely the work of John
Walker junior. In certain aspects of the formal script used for the title and
compass points (particularly the capitals M and E), one may, however, as in
the map of Chignall of 1599 (No. 10), glimpse the work of the father,
though the variations of this particular hand used at differing times by the
two men make certainty difficult.

Plate XII shows the only buildings depicted on the map.

12.—DANBURY, PURLEIGH AND   **[E.R.O., D/DU 28/59]**
WOODHAM FERRERS, *c*.1600

47.7 × 48.3cm. (18 × 19in.), parchment. Condition: good.

Title
A true platt and Contente of the Messuage and landes Called Jacklets, being the Landes of Thomas Mildmay, Esquire.

Surveyor
[John Walker senior and junior.]

Scale
No scale or scale bar given [about 4ch. to 1in. (20in. to 1m.)].

Area mapped
174 acres in extreme S.E. of Danbury, whole of former detached portion 'no. 3' of Purleigh, and N.E. of Woodham Ferrers.

Commissioned by
Thomas Mildmay.

Comment
The original lettering on the map is unmistakably that of John Walker junior, with the exception of an unnamed 'Wood' and 'springs', which are in the hand of John Walker senior. Later alterations and additions were made in the early and late 18th century. An endorsement in an early 18th century hand, now only wholly legible with the aid of ultra-violet light, reads 'Jackletts and the woods supposed to be taken in the year 1600 because the same John Walker survey'd Walton's [No. 11] for ye Same T. Mildmay Esq. in the year 1600 as may be seen by the Plot'.

Apart from Jackletts (Plate XII), the only other building shown on the map is a single-storeyed thatched cottage.

13.—STOCK AND WEST   **[E.R.O., D/DP P7]**
HANNINGFIELD, *c*.1600

20.3 × 54.6cm. (8 × 21½in.), parchment. Condition: good.

Title
The Description of the Slete al[ia]s the Sleve beginge p[ar]cell of the waste grounds belonge to Crondon Mannor.

Surveyor
[John Walker senior.]

Scale
No scale or scale bar given [about 3ch. to 1in. (about 26.6in. to 1m.)].

Area mapped
About ½-mile stretch of road from Chelmsford to Stock and land immediately adjoining.

Commissioned by
[Sir John Petre.]

Comment
The map was prepared, again no doubt for Sir John Petre, to record the relatively wide expanse of roadside waste on either side of part of the highway from Chelmsford to Stock (see Plate XIII).

Although unsigned and undated, it is unmistakably the work of John Walker senior. The lettering is less well done than in his earlier maps and perhaps indicates that his hands had suddenly grown less steady. The paramount part played by John Walker junior in the map of Chignall, 1599 (No. 10), and, as has been seen (p.36) in all the later 'joint' maps, makes this a possibility and perhaps indicates that this map slightly antedates that of Chignall, though not that of West Horndon, etc., 1598 (No. 9), which still reveals the older man at his best.

14.—WEST HANNINGFIELD, 1601*　　　　[E.R.O., D/DZt 5]

40.6×118.1cm. (16×46½in.), parchment (two conjoined skins of unequal area). Condition: the map has been badly affected by water and damp in the bottom right-hand corner and along the whole of the lower edge, where the border has at sometime been trimmed away, probably in this century when the map was mounted in a folder of buckram bound boards.

Title
Peuerells Haule or The Mannor of Peuerells in Westhanningfielde.

Surveyors
Surveyed and Measured a[nn]o D[omi]ni (1601 by John)* [Walker senior and John Walker junior].**

*Legible only with ultraviolet light.
**Illegible, names supplied.

Scale
No scale or scale bar given [3ch. to 1in. (26.6in. to 1m.)].

Area mapped
304 acres in N. and NE. of parish.

Commissioned by
John Tanfield, esquire.

Comment
Fortunately the mapped area and the principal 'Table' are unaffected by the damage detailed above, but much of another lengthy descriptive note, the date and the surname of the surveyors can no longer be read, even with the aid of ultraviolet light. The map is misdated 1611 in the *Catalogue of Maps in the Essex Record Office, Second Supplement* (1964).

The map must surely, however, have borne the names of John Walker senior and junior, for unlike all the others bearing both names this is truly a map which they jointly brought to its finished state. There can be no doubt that the older man lettered the field and other place-names (*cf.* Plates VII, VIII, noting, for example, particularly the distinctive form of letter 'g'), while his son provided the title, four compass points and principal descriptive 'Table' in his best formal text hands, and the other descriptive notes in his graceful Italic. The 'carbon copy' nature of their draughtsmanship makes it impossible to say with certainty which of them delineated the mapped area, the buildings and other features. At best, one can say, unscientifically, that in this respect the map has the 'feel' of the older man's work.

Plates XIII, XIV, reproduces all buildings.

15.—INGATESTONE, 1601   [E.R.O., D/DP P8]

177.2×135.9cm. (69$\frac{3}{4}$×53$\frac{1}{2}$in.), parchment (four conjoined skins of unequal area). Condition: the head of the map has suffered damage including abrasion as a result of being the outer layer of a roll and there has been some shelling elsewhere on the map (now arrested); otherwise good.

Title
The Mannor of Inge Petre alias Ingatestone.

Surveyors
Surveyed Measured and taken for the right Worshipful Sir John Petre knight by John Walker the elder and John Walker the younger.

Scale
Scale bar of 6in. to 96p. (20in. to 1m.).

Area mapped
2,115 acres, comprising the whole parish (including former detached part) of Ingatestone, except SE. corner [see No. 17].

Commissioned by
[See *Surveyors.*]

Comment
This large, splendid map is the earliest surviving to bear the name of both father and son, but a close comparison with the maps of White Roothing, 1609 (No. 20), and Andover (Foxcott), 1614 (No. 22), which bear the name of the latter only, proves conclusively that the lettering is wholly by the hand of the younger man (*cf.* Plates XV and XVI and Plates XX and XXII); and the overall lighter touch and use of colour throughout suggests strongly that the map in its finished state is to be ascribed to him alone. The very close similarity of the draughtsmanship of the two men revealed in maps made by them individually, however, makes this difficult to prove conclusively, though the use of the first person singular in 'The Table of Directions' is perhaps further proof.

This being so, it may be said that by 1600 John Walker junior, had served his apprenticeship outstandingly, absorbing all his father's practices and techniques to a degree that made him at least his equal.

The evidential value of the map itself is supplemented by lengthy and elaborated reference tables, keyed to it by colours and/or reference letters, which provide a written survey of the individual parcels of the demesne and of the freehold, customary and copyhold lands and tenements, arranged conveniently under the different quarters of the manor. Each entry gives the name of tenant, description and quantity of the holding. It was intended to give or to add later the amount of annual quit rent due, but after the words 'and rentith to the lorde per annum' there is a blank in each case.

The map formed the substantial basis for a detailed written survey which is not in the hand of either Walker and with which they were not apparently directly associated (No. 16).

All buildings, other than those in and close to the High Street (Plate XV), are analysed in Table 6 (pp.103-4).

16.—INGATESTONE, 1602 [E.R.O., D/DP M1449]

Volume, 30.8×20.3cm. (12⅛×8in.), paper (watermark uniform throughout), parchment covers (original, inscribed on front in one hand, probably of the early 18th century, 'No. 17 Partition No. 8. Ingatestone Survey Anno. 1602 & 1694', and in other hands, none of them contemporary with the Survey, 'Survey 1602', 'No. 17. Partition No. 8' and 'Thorndon Evidence house'), 182 pages including blanks. Condition: good.

Title
Ginge Petre als. Ingatstone. The survey of the said Mannor, according to the Plott thereof made by John Walker, and delyvered to my Mr. Sir John Petre knight, this year 1602.

Summary of Contents
(i)   Copyhold (ff.lr-27v); freehold (f.29r); demesne (ff.30r-35v).
(ii) The Survey and Rentall of the said Manor Renewed at a Court of Survey holden the fifth of June and after Severall Adjournments holden the 3^d of September 1694 . . . Copyhold (ff.lr-46v); freehold (f47r); quitrental (ff.49v-50r).
(iii) At back, unnumbered folios containing the customs and liberties, 1694, of the manor of Gingpetre and the customs of Hanley Barnes, together with an index of the two surveys.

Comment
The structure of this written survey is clearly based upon the Walkers' map, a marginal sequence of letters reflecting the several reference tables on that map. Nevertheless it is not in the hand of either Walker and there is no evidence of their being directly associated with it. The wording of the title suggests that it was compiled by one of the servants of the Petre Estate and, indeed, a draft of the survey, headed 'The Survey of Ingatestone taken owte of the mapp made by John Walker' also survives among the Petre archives [E.R.O., D/DP M1327].

The title also suggests that the Walkers' work was not handed over to Sir John until the year following the completion of the actual survey. Even during that interval the names of a number of tenants had changed. The divergence between these names in the survey volume and their counterparts on the map lends weight to the supposition that its compilation was undertaken independently of the mapmakers, as do wide differences in the spelling of personal and place-names and, in places, obvious corrections in the names used on the map.

After the map of the main demesne lands was made in 1605 (No. 17), its contents too were translated into a wholly written description and added to the draft copy, but only a beginning was made with transcribing it into the fair copy.

17.—INGATESTONE AND   [Private custody]
MOUNTNESSING, 1605

67.2×79.7cm. ($26\frac{5}{16}$ × $31\frac{5}{16}$ in.), parchment. Condition: good.

Title
A trewe Platt of the Mannors of Inge Petre Hall and Bacons with the Farmes called Westlandes Lawneys and Cuttells with two other Tenements called Brownes & Bellmans.

Surveyors
John Walker senior' et John Walker junior'.

Scale
Scale bar of 3in. to 72p. (13.3in. to 1m.).

Area mapped
About 400 acres in SE. of Ingatestone and NE. of Mountnessing with a very small area in W. of Buttsbury.

Commissioned by
John Lord Petre.

Comment
Although the Walkers surveyed the greater part of the tenants' holdings and a relatively small proportion of the demesne of the Manor of Ingatestone in 1600-01, the result of which the younger man plotted so splendidly (No. 15), some four years were to elapse before the remainder of the manor's territory, principally demesne and including Ingatestone Hall, was mapped. Part of the High Street of the village was again shown revealing changes to the front elevations of some buildings. The calligraphy and no doubt the draughtsmanship are the work of John Walker junior.

Buildings other than those reproduced in Plate XVII are analysed in Table 7 (pp.105-6).

18.—MATCHING, 1609   [E.R.O., D/DU 25]

66.7×81.6cm. (26¼×32⅛in.), parchment. Condition: the right-hand and bottom borders have been trimmed away and there remains some evidence that they had been partially eaten away. The map appears to have suffered a contraction of the parchment (see *Scale*) as a result of being in an excessively dry and possibly hot environment at some time; otherwise it is in a good state.

Title
A Trewe Platt of the cheife Mannor or capitall Messuage called and knowne by the name of Househam Haule Scituate in the Parish of Matchinge in the Countie of Essex, with the Copiesholde Landes thereunto belonginge.

Surveyors
John Walker Senior & John Walker Junior.

Scale
Scale bar of 4.8(5)in. to 80p. (19.2(20)in. to 1m.).

Area mapped
415 acres in W., SW. and centre of parish.

Commissioned by
[Sir Edward Alleyn (in right of his wife Elizabeth, daughter and heir of George Scott esquire).]

Comment
Once more the overall evidence, particularly the scripts used, is that the finished map is the work of John Walker junior and this may be most strikingly seen when it is placed beside the map of White Roothing (No. 20) drawn in the same year and bearing the name of the younger man only. Both are examples of his skill and elegance scarcely surpassed by either himself or his father. The careful, restrained use of colour to denote legal boundaries is in marked contrast with the heavy-handed applications in the latest surviving maps (Nos. 26-28, Plates XXVII-XXIX). All buildings are reproduced in Plate XVIII; see also pp.91-2.

19.—LITTLE LEIGHS, 1609   [Public Record Office, MPA 24]

55.9×68.9cm. (22×27⅛in.), parchment. Condition: good.

Title
A trewe Platt of the Mannor of Little Leighes Haule within the Countie of Essex.

Surveyors
Surveyed Measured and taken by John Walker Senior and John Walker Junior.

Scale
Scale bar of 5in. to 80p. (20in. to 1m.).

Area mapped
309 acres in E. and centre of parish.

Commissioned by
[Sir Edw. Alleyn (in right of wife Elizabeth, daughter and heir of George Scott, esquire).]

Comment
Although bearing the name of father and son, the map bears all the hallmarks of John Walker junior's lettering and draughtsmanship, uniform with those of the maps of Matching and White Roothing (Nos. 18 and 20) drawn in the same year. See Plate XIX which shows all buildings except an isolated single-storey cottage.

20.—WHITE ROOTHING, 1609   [E.R.O., D/DC 27/1118]

53.6×117.2cm. (21⅛×46⅛in.), parchment (two conjoined skins of unequal area). Condition: good.

Title
A Trewe and perfect Platt of the Demeine Landes belonginge to the Mannor of Mascalls Bury, Scituate, lyinge and beinge within the Parish of white Roodinge.

Surveyor
Surveyed Measured and taken The vjth of Maye anno D[omi]ni 1609 By me John Walker Junior.

Scale
Scale bar of 5in. to 80p. (20in. to 1m.).

Area mapped
406 acres in SW., S., SE. and E. of parish.

Commissioned by
Sir John Poyntz *alias* Morris, knight.

Comment
This map, the earlier of the two to bear the name of John Walker junior only, provides the vital clues that all extant maps bearing the names of both father and son are, with one exception (No. 14), in their finished state the work of the younger man. As to the higher order of excellence of this map, there is little need to add to the *Comment* to the map of Matching (No. 18) above. All buildings are reproduced in Plates XIX, XX; see also pp.92-3.

21.—MUNDON, 1612   **[E.R.O., D/DFg P2]**

86.4×65.4cm. (34×25$\frac{3}{4}$in.), paper. Condition: apart from wear and some minor tears along folds (now flattened), good.

Title
[None]

Surveyors
Surveyed, Measured and taken by vs in September a[nn]*o* d[omi]ni 1612 by John Walker Senior and John Walker Junior.

Scale
No scale or scale bar [4ch. to 1in. (20in. to 1m.)].

Area mapped
783 acres in W., centre, SE. and E. of parish.

Commissioned by
[Unknown]

Comment
The map lacks completely colour or other embellishment, so that (although the usual care is bestowed on the front elevation of buildings) thatch and tile, etc., are not distinguished. Unlike the map of Chignall, 1599 (No. 10), there is no evidence that this is probably a draft map; indeed, the care in the lettering, which is again wholly by the hand of John Walker junior, suggests the opposite. It is the only surviving example, if this is so, of the Walkers offering 'a penny plain' on paper as well as 'a twopence coloured' on parchment to their patrons. See Plate XXI which reproduces the few buildings, including Mundon Hall and church.

22.—ANDOVER (HAMPSHIRE), 1614 [Bodleian Library, MS. Rolls Hants. 44]

227.3×67cm. ($89\frac{1}{2}$×$26\frac{3}{8}$in.), parchment (three conjoined skins of unequal area). Condition: good.

Title
A Trewe and perfect Platt of the Mannor of Fosscutt with certain other dispersed landes lyinge in Hatherden Charlton & Penton as appeareth by writinge in the last Tables in this Platt &c All which sayde Landes are Scituate lyinge and beinge in the Parish & Fields of Andeuere in the Countie of Southampton.

Surveyor
The Landes Conteyned within this Platt or Surueye lyinge within Foxcoate Hatherden Charlton and Penton [long space-filler] were Surueyed Measured and Taken in the Monethes of November and December and in the Yeare of our Lorde God. 1614. by me John Walker Juniorem.

Scale
Scale bar of 6in. to 96p. (20in. to 1m.).

Area mapped
1,175 acres in the chapelry of Foxcott and the hamlets of Hatherden, Charlton and Penton.

Commissioned by
Sir Edward Barrett, knight.

Comment

The only known example of a survey carried out by either of the Walkers beyond the borders of Essex must be reckoned as one of the finest maps drawn by the son. The special problems of surveying a 'champion' and heavily wooded region are coped with as well as with any 'enclosed' estate in Essex. In working outside his native county for a new patron the younger Walker may well have felt that he was particularly on his mettle and consequently exercised greater care in representing all detail. The amount of space available to contain the very lengthy tables largely recording the individual strips in the common fields was nicely calculated, so that the writing does not deteriorate in size and quality, as is the case with the maps of Stock and Buttsbury, 1616, and Springfield, c.1616 (Nos. 26 and 28).

The first explanatory 'Table' is perhaps the best example of the graceful, scholarly English employed by the Walkers and provides us with the best expression of their dedication and intent (see below).

All buildings are reproduced in Plate XXII.

Transcription of 'The first Table or Index'

Forasmuch as it is a thinge vsuall amongest manie Surveyours, and also in my Judgement most necessarie & needefull first to sett downe some direcc[i]ons to be as it were a Lanthorne and light for the Lord or Owner of the landes of which any Survey is made of for the readier and easier findinge out of any thinge in the sayde Survey that they doe desier. I therefore right worshippfull haue here vnto this my Survey of the Mannor of Foscutt added this Table or Index with a second Table followeinge. in this first declaringe the scituac[i]on of the sayd Mannor with the Landes Tenementes and Hereditaments therevnto belonginge where and in what Parish and Countie they lye in & with manie other matters as hereafter followeth, in the second naminge euery perticuler Tennaunte houldinge any of the sayde landes, whither Demeine or copie, and also sheweinge what quantitie any one of them houlde. vizt what landes any of the sayd Tennauntes hould aswell in any common fielde as in other growndes belonginge to the sayd Mannor demeine or copie with other matters as appeareth in the syad Table as with what coloures any mans lande is shadowed withall and with what letters signed &c. Which sayd Mannor of Foscutt beinge the Inheritaunce of the right worshippfull Sir Edwarde Barrett Knight is scituate lyinge and beinge in the parish and fieldes of Andeuere in the Countie of Southampton in a verie healthsome soyle havinge a Chappell belonginge vnto it, and lyeth betweene two Mannors vizt the Mannor of Penton and the Mannor of Charlton extendinge in length from Abbott Sande common fieldes to the Parish and fieldes of Tangley beinge a thinge verie well wooded and partelie for the most parte reasonable good lande as that Quarter doth afforde, The woodes and landes called Dynes lyeth betweene two Heathes vizt Hatherden Heath and Charlton al[ia]s Dowles Heath which two Heathes abutteth vpon two Forrestes to witt the Forrest of Chute the Kinges maiesties lyinge or abuttinge vpon $\overset{e}{y}$ edge of Wiltshire, and the forrest of Dowles the Lord Marques All which sayde Mannor landes, arable, pasture, meadowes and woodes with the Sheepedowne aswell the copie lands as demeines howsoeuer they lye dispersed ether about Fosscutt or Hatherden belonginge to the sayde Mannor in common or otherwise are sett forth in true and iust proportion with euerie, Gate, Style Pathe, Ponde, Brooke, Bridge, Highwayes and Driftewayes leadinge into through or by any parte peece or percell of the sayde landes demeine or copie with the mannor house scituated and placed in the right place with the edifices thervnto belonginge and all the other Tenementes & Heriditam^{ts} either about Fosscutt Streate or Hatherden in there iust and right places with all the edifices belonginge to any or either of them, the Chappell also beinge sett forth in his right place, and also all the rowes and hedgerowes belonginge to any of the sayde landes demeine or copie as in the Platt yt doeth and may more at large and plainely appeare. Furthermore yow shall finde written in euerie enclosed fielde, close, or woode the most knowne names and also in euerie sayd percell or other peices lyinge in common or otherwise the true contentes of acres, roodes and perches with $\overset{e}{y}$ names of the Tennauntes houldinge any copie peece within anie of the sayd common fieldes &c. Moreouer I haue also added another Table for the landes lyinge in Charlton mannor with the true contentes therof and how they butt and bound vpon other mens landes as they lye dispersed in diuerse filedes within the sayde mannor, Also I haue sett downe in another place by it selfe the landes lyinge in $\overset{e}{y}$ mannor of Penton with the contentes and buttalls therof as they lye dispersed and in $\overset{e}{y}$ ende a generall content of $\overset{e}{y}$ whole as in the Platt and by the Tables all thinges in this Table mentioned doeth more at large and plainely appeare &c.

Finis

23.—EAST, WEST AND SOUTH HANNINGFIELD, 1614   [E.R.O., D/DP M890]

Volume, 29.8×20cm. (11¾×7⅞in.), paper (watermark uniform throughout), original vellum covers embellished back and front in gold with a tooled light outer frame and an inner frame with floral motifs at the corners and a large central motif of conventional flowers and foliage; 68 pages including blanks. Condition: good, except for insect borings through paper close to binding.

Title
A Booke of Survey of the Mannors of Easte Weste and Southanningfield.

Surveyors
Taken And made Anno Domini 1614 by John Walker senior' and John Walker Junior'.

Summary of Contents
(i) 'The Table', i.e., an index to holdings and tenants (4pp., unnumbered, preceding title page).
(ii) 'A Surueye of the Freehouldes houlden of the right Honourable the Lord Burgauenie of his aforesaide Mannor of Easte Westhanningfielde' (pp.1-5).
(iii) 'Here followeth The Freeholde Landes houlden of the Mannor of Southanningfielde Hall' (pp.6-7).
(iv) 'A Contente of the Copieshoulde Landes in Easte Weste= hanningfielde & first in Westhan(n)ingfielde' (pp.11-22).
(v) 'Eastehanningfielde Copieholdes' (pp.23-33).
(vi) 'Southanningfielde Copieholders' (pp.34-36).
(vii) 'A Pertition Made in Marche Anno Domini. 1615.' (p.37). (See *Comment* below.)
[There are no maps.]

Commissioned by
Edward Nevill, Lord Abergavenny.

Comment
Although this written survey is so close in date to the maps of 1615 (Nos. 24 and 25), neither makes reference to the other, though the note of a partition of one holding (vii) was almost certainly added in consequence of the resurvey for the maps. This note, as is the whole volume, is in the hand of John Walker junior. See Plate XXII for an illustration of the detailed nature of the survey.

24.—EAST HANNINGFIELD, 1615   [E.R.O., D/DP P10]

142.2×94cm. (56×37in.), parchment (four conjoined skins of unequal area). Condition: good except for some rubbing away of the left-hand border.

Title
A Trewe and perfect Platt of the Mannor of Eastwesthanningfielde . . .*

Surveyors
Surveyed Measured and taken in Maye Anno Domini 1615 by vs John Walker seniorem and John Walker junior'.

Scale
Scale bar of 4in. to 64p. (20in. to 1m.).

Area mapped
737 acres, comprising the whole parish of East Hanningfield except N., NE. and extreme SW. (657 acres), extreme E. of West Hanningfield (48 acres) and extreme NE. of Downham (32 acres).

Commissioned by
Edward Nevill, Lord Abergavenny.

Comment
The presence of the name of John Walker senior, on the map is again to be taken as acknowledgement only of his part in carrying out the field work, for by the criteria already established the map itself is the work of his son and may perhaps be reckoned among his best. Certainly, it provides the finest example of his calligraphy and the drawing of front elevations of buildings show an unsurpassed attention to detail (see Plate XXIV). The 'first Table or Index' makes mention of a 'second Platt' of the Manor of South Hanningfield, which is discussed in the next entry. All buildings are analysed in Table 8.

There is no cross-reference to the written survey of 1614 (No. 23), nor indeed any mention of it on the map.

25.—SOUTH HANNINGFIELD, *c.*1615   [E.R.O., D/DP P11]

55.2×42.9cm. (21¾×16⅞in.), parchment. Condition: good.

Title
[None]

*The introductory words of 'The first Table or Index'.

Surveyor
[Not stated. See *Comment* below.]

Scale
Scale bar of 4½in. to 108p. (numbered only to 72) (13.3in. to 1m.).

Area mapped
About 430 acres in centre, NE., E. and SE. of parish.

Commissioned by
Edward Nevill, Lord Abergavenny.

Comment
A 'platt' of South Hanningfield is mentioned in 'The first Table or Index' of the map of East Hanningfield, 1615 (No. 24), and although this map is undated, the internal evidence confirms a dating of *c.*1615. It has clearly something of the style of John Walker senior and junior, but just as clearly, upon closer examination, it is the finished work of neither father nor son, though certain aspects of the handwriting owe something to both, particularly the latter. The most obvious difference from their work is the representation of buildings (except South Hanningfield church) in perspective and there is nothing to suggest that accurate, detailed drawings were intended (see Plate XXVI); field boundaries are characteristically represented by a green band, but there is no underlying black line; the elementary mistake, *Scala Perticaram (sic),* above the scale bar may be significant; such error is not to be found on any other map drawn and lettered by John Walker junior who favoured these Latin words.

The possibility that the map may be the first known example of the work of Samuel Walker* immediately springs to mind. His surviving maps of Good Easter, 1623 (No. 30), and Little Dunmow, 1631 (No. 33), offer little obvious support for this, for they both show that by the date of the earlier he had adopted for his estate plans a bold, flamboyant style, particularly in the lettering, distinctively his own.

That the handwriting on this map may be, nevertheless, by his hand is strongly supported by his written survey of the Manors of East West Hanningfield and South Hanningfield made in 1628 (see Plate XXXIII and *cf.* Plate XXIV). In which case, as the rest of the map, although stylistically similar to their work, is not by either John Walker senior or junior, it is not unreasonable to accept that the map is wholly by Samuel and perhaps to

*See p.25 above for discusion of his relationship to John Walker senior and junior.

regard it as an example of his work as an apprentice to them. The disappointingly conventional treatment of buildings remains, however, puzzling, for his later maps demonstrate that in their representation, at least, he followed the practice of the two Johns.

It remains possible that the map is a copy of one by John junior made by Samuel as an apprentice's exercise on a reduced scale, but its presence in the Petre archives with that of East Hanningfield militates against this.

26.—STOCK AND BUTTSBURY, 1616   [E.R.O., D/DMa P1]

61×57.1cm. ($24 \times 22\frac{1}{2}$in.), parchment. Condition: the map has suffered considerably from damp and abrasion and parts are legible only with the aid of an ultraviolet light source. There has been a degree of contraction of the parchment (see *Scale*).

Title
A Trewe and perfect Platt of the two Mannors of Whites and Ramseys . . .*

Surveyor
Johannes Walker hoc descripsit Mense Augustij Anno Domini. 1616.

Scale
Scale bar of $2\frac{7}{8}$(3)in. to 60p. (15.3(16)in. to 1m.).

Area mapped
530 acres in centre, N. and W. of Stock and NW. and N. of Buttsbury.

Commissioned by
Sir John Tyrrell, knight.

Comment
Although the name Johannes Walker appears on the map without qualification, the lettering shows it to be the work of John Walker junior. (See Plate XXVII and *cf.* Plates XIX, XX and XXII.) It is one of the less pleasing maps, for the lettering is rather less carefully done than usual and the application of colour, particularly to denote legal boundaries, is too heavily and hastily applied. The blank spaces left after the drawing of the

*The introductory words of 'The First Table'.

map provide insufficient room to record all the written information comfortably and in part of one reference table the writing becomes progressively smaller and more currently written. The buildings, however, are as carefully treated as ever. For an analysis of all buildings, see Table 9 (p.109).

27.—TOLLESHUNT D'ARCY AND TOLLESHUNT MAJOR, 1616 [British Library, Maps 2420 (7)]

[50.8×63.5cm. (20×25in.), parchment.] Original now lost (see below).

Title
A trewe and perfect Platt of the cheife Messuage and la(n)ds with the wasted Farme houses as were late Master Stephen Bekinghams Esquyer and now the Landes and Farmes of the worshippfull Master Stephen Bekingham . . .*

Surveyor
Surveyed Measured and taken Anno Domini. 1616. by me John Walker.

Scale
Scale bar of 3in. to 48p. (20in. to 1m.).

Area mapped
266 acres in W. of Tollehunt D'Arcy (including S. half of former detached part 'no. 1' of parish) and E. of Tolleshunt Major.

Comment
As in the case of the map of Stock and Buttsbury (No. 26), the name of John Walker is here unqualified, but all the lettering is by the hand of John junior. The overall treatment is more heavy-handed than in his best work, being again accentuated by the excessively thick bands of colour to denote legal boundaries.

The whereabouts of the original map is no longer known. It was extant in 1925 when it was photographed by the Ordnance Survey, but there is no record of its custodian at that time. It is listed in the Ordnance Survey's *A Catalogue of Photographs of Old Cadastral and Other Plans of Great Britain,* Southampton, 1935. The photograph was destroyed when the O.S. office was bombed during the Second World War, but fortunately a duplicate had

*Introductory words of 'The Table of Index'.

been deposited in the British Museum. From the photographic print (reproduced as Plate XXVII), it can be seen that the original map had most regrettably been dissected and mounted on linen.

28.—SPRINGFIELD, *c*.1616   [E.R.O., D/DGe P2/1]

76.2×105.4cm. (30×41$\frac{1}{2}$in.), parchment. Condition: the map has been grievously damaged in parts by water and most of the tables are illegible without the aid of an ultraviolet light source.

Title
A New and perfect Platt of the Mannors of Springfielde Hall and Dukes . . .*

Surveyors
John Walker senior and John Walker junior.

Scale
Scale bar of 6in. to 96p. (20in. to 1m.).

Area mapped
547 acres in centre and W. and scattered parts of E. of parish.

Commissioned by
Sir John Tyrrell, knight.

Comment
In the last surviving map to bear the names of both John Walker senior and John Walker junior one is again looking at the draughtsmanship and calligraphy of the younger man, though in common with the two other maps of 1616 it exhibits a sad decline in his standards. The whole map, except in the representation of buildings, lacks finish and the usual great care. Its general appearance (see Plates XXVIII, XXIX) is made even less attractive by the use of rather muddy red and green colours and an unfortunate application of other dense colours to mark legal boundaries already seen in the two maps dated 1616 (Nos. 26 and 27, Plate XXVII).

The damage to the map noted above must have largely, if not wholly, occurred after 1830 when David Wood, a Chelmsford surveyor, made two

---

*Introductory words of 'The First Table'.

copies of the map transcribing the reference tables in full, though the date was presumably already difficult to read, since he rendered it as 1514 [D/DGe P2/2].

The date 1604 has also been previously assigned to the map *(Catalogue of Maps in the Essex Record Office, 1566-1855* 1947), but this is supported neither by the use of ultraviolet light, under which it remains illegible, nor by internal and external evidence. Analysis of the court roll of the Manors of Springfield Hall and Dukes, 1603-1625 [D/DGe M100], reveals that some of the manorial tenants named on the map were admitted to their holdings some years after 1604 and one indeed as late as the beginning of 1617. The deterioration of John Walker junior's work seen here must associate the map with the two of 1616 (Nos. 26 and 27) and it is likely to have been commissioned by Sir John Tyrrell at much the same time as the first of these.

All buildings are analysed in Table 10 (p.110).

29.—HIGH EASTER, GREAT DUNMOW AND GREAT WALTHAM, 1622   [British Library, Add. MS. 41848]

59.3 × 78.8cm. ($23\frac{11}{16}$ × $31\frac{1}{2}$in.), parchment. Condition: good.

Title
A true and perfect Plott of all the Demesne Landes belonging to the Mannor of Garnetts, Scituate, lying and being in the seuerall Parrishes of High Easter, Dunmowe Magna and Waltham Magna in the Countie of Essex. Hauing the Priuiledg of keeping Courte Barron, With the proffitts and comodities therevnto beelonging of Free and Customarie lands. Viz. Quitt Rents, Releeses, Fynes, Waifes, Strayes, Deodants, Hawking, Hunting, Fishing and Fowling &c. The Chappell, Mansion house and other ten[ement]s in their true places and order, Euerie Gatehouse, Barnes, Stables, Douehouse, Orchards, Yardes, Gardens, highwaies, Driftwaies, Ponds, Pathes, Pound, Stiles, Gates, Bridges. And euery particuler Fielde, Woods, Springs, Hedg rowes, placed in their right Formes. With the Contents of Acres, Roodes and Perches of euery Seuerall, As in this Plott most plainlie it doth appeare.

Surveyor
Measured and Suruayed in Anno D[omi]ni, 1622. By mee Samuel Walker.

Scale
Scale bar. 'Scaled after 16 Rods to the Inche' (20in. to 1m.).

Area mapped
449a. 1r. 4p., mostly in north of parish of High Easter.

Commissioned by
Sir William Fitch.

Comment
The representation of features, above all of buildings, clearly shows (Plate XXX) the development of Samuel Walker as a former pupil of John Walker senior and junior, and as a true, if lesser, heir of their style and tradition. Only in calligraphy had he developed a less elegant, more flamboyant style of his own, although the words incorporated in his scale show that he had not forgotten a fair italic hand, perhaps learnt from John Walker junior.

All buildings on the original map are illustrated on Plate XXX, apart from one tiled, single-storeyed cottage, and one small tiled barn.

30.—GOOD EASTER, 1623   [E.R.O., D/DU 28/60]

71.7×61.5cm. (28¼×24¼in.), parchment. Condition: badly creased and faded along the centre and edges following damage from damp; repaired in parts.

Title
A true and perfect Plott of all the demesne lands belonging to the Capitall Messuages, or Fermes, called ye Prebendens commonly knowne by the seuerall distinct names of Falconers hall, Burrowes, In-birdes, and Parslowes. With ye true scituations of the Church Mansion howses, Barnes, Stables, Pondes, Stiles, Gates, Rivers, High-waies, Drift-Waies, and every particuler fielde or close in their true forme and order as they now lye. And lastly ye contents of euerie seuerall fielde or close sett downe in Figures at length: In ye first place Acres: the second Roodes: and ye third Perches.

Surveyor
Measured, and Survayed in Anno Domini 1623 by Samuell Walker.

Scale
Scale bar of 4in. to 64p. (20in. to 1m.).

Area mapped
447 acres in W. and centre of parish.

Commissioned by
[Sir Henry Mildmay, kt., of Graces in Little Baddow.]

Comment
See comment for High Easter, 1622 (No. 29). All buildings on the orginal map are illustrated on Plate XXXI.

31.—WICKHAM BISHOPS, 1624   [E.R.O., Acc.6148: D/DMg]

81.0×67.2cm. (31$\frac{7}{8}$×26$\frac{1}{2}$in.), parchment. Condition: the left-hand margin has been damaged by fire leaving a series of semi-circular indentations to a depth of some 5cm. Only a few words of text and scarcely any of the mapped area are affected. Otherwise, sound.

Title
A true and perfect Plott, or Particuler demonstration of all and singuler the arrable, pasture, and meadowe landes: being part of the demesnes belonging to the Mannor of Wickham hall; Scituate in the parrish of Wickham in the Countie of Essex . . .

Surveyor
Measured and Survayed, Anno Domini 1624, By mee, Samuell Walker.

Scale
Scale bar. 'Scaled after 16 Rodes to the Inche' (20in. to 1m.).

Area mapped
525 acres in W. and SW. of parish.

Commissioned by
[Uncertain: see *Comment*.]

Comment
As with the 1623 map of Good Easter (No. 30) to which stylistically this is almost a twin, one could not mistake the influence of John Walker senior and junior, in the careful depiction of buildings in elevation (Plate XXXII). In other aspects, however, Samuel shows himself to be far more eclectic in his use of decorative elements. The depiction of a fish in a pond; the border, decorated with a series of semi-circles, triangles and other geometrical shapes, in a variety of irregularly used colours; and the elaborate decoration of initial letters, at one place erupting into a human profile, show a

flamboyance bordering on lack of restraint, a preoccupation with the parts rather than the whole, which the two Johns would never have allowed themselves.

The estate here mapped was the property of the Bishop of London and in the tenure of William, Lord Maynard. Which of the two commissioned the map is uncertain but the balance of probability seems to favour the Maynards, as being more likely both to favour the local mapmaker and to require a single parchment map rather than a bound survey-format.

The only buildings not shown on Plate XXXII are the parish church and the priest's house nearby.

32.—EAST, WEST AND SOUTH HANNINGFIELD, 1628   [E.R.O., D/DP M1521]

Volume, 28.6×19cm. (11¼×7½in.), paper (watermark uniform throughout), original vellum covers embellished front and back in gold with a tooled light frame and a central motif consisting of a quartered diamond shape conventionally decorated and with the letters H B respectively on either side; 62 ff. including blanks.

Title
A true Booke wherein is conteyned a perfect Demonstration of all the Customarie, and Freehouldes within the seuerall Mannours of Easte, West, and South Han[n]ingfield in the County of Essex; With their seuerall Contents, Tenures: Number of Acres: Quitt-Rentes, Herriotts and yearely valew of Each of them: Togither with the Names and Sirnames of all the Tennants now liuinge. Which said Seuerall Mannours are the Possessions of the Right Honnorable the Lord Henry; Lord Abergaueney./

Surveyor
Carefullie and faithfully Surueyed and delineated according to Arte: By Samuell Walker. Anno Domini. 1628./

Summary of Contents
(i)   Manor of East West Hanningfield: copyhold or customary holdings (ff.1-28).
(ii)   'Heere followe the Freehouldes of the Manno(u)r of East and West Hanningfield' (ff.29-37).
(iii) 'The Manno(u)r; of Sowth: Hanningfield = Hall: Being A Mannour of it Selfe; And hath the same prefects the other Mannour hath. And first of the Coppie Houldes to the same Mannour beelonginge./.' (ff.39-44).

(iv) 'Heere followe the Freehoulds of the Mannor of South=
hanningfielde' (ff.45-49).

(v) 'The table, or Index of the whole Booke' (ff.51-55). (Not arranged
alphabetically by tenants' names but in precisely the same order as
they appear in the survey.)

Commissioned by
[See *Title*.]

Comment
This detailed written survey offers better evidence than his maps that
Samuel Walker, whatever his family relationship to them, was a pupil or
apprentice of John Walker senior and junior. The general style of his
handwriting resembles strikingly that of the younger John and offers the
best evidence that the map of South Hanningfield, *c.*1615 (No. 25), may
well be his work. See Plate XXXIII.

33.—LITTLE DUNMOW, 1631   [E.R.O., D/DYu 2]

52.1×70.5cm. (20½×27¾in.), parchment.

Title
The Plott or Description of the Mannor of Dunmow Priory within the
Parish of Dunmow Parva.

Surveyor
Measd [*sic*] and: Survayed By Samuell Walker ./. Anno Domini. 1631-.

Scale
'Scaled after Sixteene Rods to the Inche' (20in. to 1m.).

Area mapped
249 acres in centre of parish.

Commissioned by
[Edward, Earl of Sussex.]

Comment
In this map Samuel Walker continues the 'Walker' practice of representing
buildings by their front elevations, but has abandoned the use of red to

denote tile or brick. The secular buildings are probably reasonably accurate, but the drawing of Little Dunmow church bears little relationship to the actual building. The lettering of the field-names is less ornate than that on the map of Good Easter, 1623, but is ungainly in appearance, mainly because of the long upright ascenders. See Plate XXIV.

34.—MOUNTNESSING, 1622   [E.R.O., D/DP P12]

57.5×66.3cm. (22⅝×26⅛in.), parchment. Condition: good.

Title
The Mannor of Mountneysinge Hall.

Surveyor
Andrew Pease.

Scale
Scale bar of 2⅞(3)in. to 48p. (19.8(20)in. to 1m.).

Area mapped
418 acres in E. centre of parish.

Commissioned by
[William Lord Petre.]

Comment
This is the only known map which may be by another apprentice or pupil of the Walkers or by someone closely connected with them. Although there is no pictorial treatment of physical boundaries, except the representation of trees as in the case of the majority of Walker maps, the delineation of buildings in elevation (though markedly inferior), the restrained use of colour, the scale simply represented by a pair of dividers surmounting a rule, and the neat lettering, particularly the Italic of the few field-names given, reminiscent of John Walker junior, are suggestive. It is altogether a well-drawn map (Plate XXXIV).

Andrew Pease had good opportunity to learn from the Walkers, for he was clerk of the kitchen to Sir John (later 1st Lord) Petre and later appears to have become chief steward of the same household in succession to his father-in-law, John Bentley, who died in 1597.

35.—LAINDON, 1705 [E.R.O., D/DU 64]

62.4×55.2cm. (26×23in.), parchment. Condition: good.

Title
A Trewe and Perfect Platt of the Mannor of Lainedon Hall being the Inheritance of James Harris yeoman.

Surveyor
[See *Comment*.]

Scale
Scale bar of 5in. to 80p. (20in. to 1m.).

Area mapped
221 acres in S. centre of parish.

Commissioned by
[Unknown.]

Comment
This map (Plate XXXV) is almost certainly evidence of a lost work by either John Walker senior or junior. The style of the map in draughtsmanship and language is clearly archaic for the early 18th century and with the lengthy tables is very suggestive of that of the Walkers; the draughtsman is careful to state 'Drawn (not surveyed) by John Friend'. Moreover, James Harris named as the owner of the estate in 'The First Table' appears frequently in the Essex Quarter Sessions Rolls between 1590 and 1617, variously described as yeoman or gentleman; and Anthony Pake also named in the same 'Table' is referred to at Broomfield in 1605. Friend has only allowed his individuality to show in the compasses surmounting the scale. The map is therefore illustrative of Laindon at least a century before the date appearing on it.

The value of Walker maps as an aid to the study of secular buildings

Over the past twenty years or more, the drawings of buildings on Walker maps have proved to be a reliable aid to the study of architecture in Essex and, particularly, vernacular architecture.

Many early estate cartographers and other mapmakers have embellished their maps with drawings of buildings. Some of these drawings are conventional; they give no indication of a building's true appearance. Other mapmakers, including Israel Amyce and Ralph Treswell, intended their drawings to be representational, but all of them were faced with the difficulty of giving verisimilitude to small drawings, even to a mapmaker working on a scale of as much as 4 chains to the inch. This was a pity: there are a fair number of well-executed Elizabethan estate maps still surviving, and in not one seen so far, apart from those by the Walkers, do the drawings of buildings match the standard of the lettering, decoration and draughtsmanship. This is true even of maps by the famous Ralph Agas.

There was one other cartographical way of depicting buildings. This is seen on the well-known Elizabethan 'maps' of London and other cities. These are really bird's-eye views. The London series—Braun and Hogenberg, the so-called 'Agas' and others—are all derived from a 'map', now lost, apart from two of its engraved copper plates, each $11\frac{3}{4}$ by $19\frac{3}{4}$ inches, out of a total of probably 15, to make a map 3 feet 8 inches by 7 feet 5 inches. One of the plates is the subject of an absorbing and gracefully written monograph by Stephen Powys Marks.[1] It covers the area around Moorfields, and is superior to any of its Elizabethan successors; there seems to be no doubt that the buidlings depicted are accurate representations. All these bird's-eye views, however, have one serious defect—a bird looks only in the direction in which it is flying. When a street faces a bird it presents a perfect front view of one of its sides, while it is possible to see the interesting structural features of the backs of the houses on the other side of that street. But when the street is end-on to the bird, there is not much joy for modern students of ancient buildings!

The Walkers produced true plans of estates, not bird's-eye views. They also refrained, with rare exceptions, from depicting buildings in normal perspective; they drew front elevations with the baselines always in their correct positions. This method had obvious disadvantages; they could not show ends of buildings and could give no hint of back gables and short back wings, although long back wings (see Chelmsford, 1591, Plate V) and courtyard houses (see Moulsham, 1591, Plate VII and Chelmsford, 1591, Plate V) *could* be depicted. Their method also produced optical effects which seem strange to anyone seeing a Walker map for the first time: all buildings appear to have been bent over from the front and flattened into the ground; while the Walkers' admirable insistence on showing the true baseline leads to some odd-looking results, especially in a farm complex (Plate XVIII), where house, stables, barns, oxhouses and cartsheds face in many different directions, as, indeed, they did in fact!

But their method possessed a decided advantage over drawings in perspective. It was the only way by which a town street could be depicted in accurate profile. This has been proved by careful comparison of Walker maps with the 25-inch Ordnance Survey, and particularly by the projection of *slides* of Walker detail on the 25-inch map; while Miss Hilda Grieve in her researches into the history of Chelmsford found Walker's map of 1591 to be an absolutely dependable jumping-off point (see Note 16).

The reliability of the Walkers can be demonstrated most fully in their drawings of *mansions,* alas, very few in number. These, on the Walkers' usual scale of 20 inches to one mile, are an inch or more in width, large enough for a considerable amount of detail to be shown. In most examples of vernacular architecture—of humbler buildings—this degree of detail was not possible; here, they were not even thumbnail sketches—it would be quite possible to place four or six drawings on one average thumbnail. However, it will be shown below, that when the Walkers drew, say, a hall-house with an open hall, one two-storeyed crosswing to its left, an off-centre chimney stack and an off-centre front door, then these features were present in the actual house and in those positions. Moreover, the width of the drawing, even if less than $\frac{1}{4}$-inch, could be related with reasonable confidence to the scale and thus to the width of the building itself. The Walkers added some valuable bonuses: they always distinguished between tile and thatch and between plain brick and plastered timber-framing or brickwork. They also depicted those fairly rare examples where the timber-framing was still exposed externally. Incidentally, they had one amazing failing: they often exaggerated their chimney stacks and especially the capping; but in their actual building most Elizabethans seem to have gone slightly crazy about stacks!

The most convenient starting point for proving the Walkers' reliability is Old West Horndon (or Thorndon) Hall, near Brentwood, since this can be checked against some other remarkable documentary evidence. The mansion was built of brick *c.* 1415, by Lewis John, founder of the FitzLewes family,[2] and was enlarged in the mid-15th century to give a frontage of about 260 feet.[3] It passed by marriage to the Mordaunt family and was bought from them in 1573 by Sir John Petre, afterwards John, 1st Lord

Petre.[4] Between *c.*1575 and *c.*1595, it was considerably remodelled by Sir John; the progress of the rebuilding can be followed fairly well as, fortunately, the very detailed annual building accounts for five separate years have been preserved, and these are spread evenly over the period.[5] When the work was completed, Sir John commissioned John Walker senior, to produce his fine map and survey, 1598, of West Horndon manor and adjacent Petre estates, including a drawing of the Hall and its outbuildings.[6] This map and a drawing to illustrate *The Travels by Cosmo the Third, Grand Duke of Tuscany, in England,* 1669, are the only surviving representations of Old Thorndon Hall. By the early 18th century, the building was in poor condition and probably ill-suited to Georgian ways of living. In 1733, the young 8th Lord Petre, the eminent botanist, engaged Giacomo Leoni to refurbish and partly rebuild it. The elaborate scheme was never completed; it was cut short in 1742 when the 8th Lord died of small-pox in his 30th year. Leoni's plans of the Old Hall and of the projected remodelling have survived;[7] so, too, has an exceptionally fine map of 1733, showing the proposed layout of the environs.[8] In 1763, the 9th Lord Petre completely demolished the Old Hall and built a classical mansion to the designs of James Paine and on a new site a mile and a quarter to the north.

Walker's drawing (Plate X) can be related closely to the Elizabethan building accounts, to the Cosmo drawing and to Leoni's plans. Leoni shows that the main block of the mansion had a frontage of 266 feet and half an inch. Walker's drawing of it is $1\frac{1}{3\frac{1}{2}}$ inches in width. This, set against the scale, gives a frontage of $272\frac{1}{4}$ feet, a negligible margin of error, where the stroke of a pen would be equivalent to about two feet. All the main features of the mansion are shown: the High Tower and the Bell Tower with their lead cappings; the Great Tower with its battlements; the hall and its porch, recessed behind the terrace; steps leading down to the gatehouse courtyard; the many windows, gables and tall chimneys. Behind, and to the north-east, is an L-shaped building, the bakehouse with its Clock Tower and one range of stables; this was built in 1589-90.[9] To the east is the massive block of farm buildings (barn, more stables, saddlehouse and slaughterhouse), built also in 1589-90. North of it is the large enclosure for 'strangers' horses'. To the north-west of the mansion is the Great Garden, with its 'vault' (the water-supply) in the centre and the banqueting house in the north-west angle. Westwards is the orchard; southwards is the gatehouse and, beyond it, West Horndon church.

Three detailed examples should put the veracity of Walker beyond all doubt. The collection of buildings at West Horndon gives a predominant effect of redness, of Elizabethan brick and tile. But Walker shows that the gatehouse range was built partly of brick, partly of stone. The building accounts for 1593-94[10] confirm this: the stone came by sea from Beer in Devon to the wharf at Grays, Essex, and the masons' work was carried out by Daniel Kettle of Aldersgate Street and his team. The appearance of the gatehouse as shown by Walker tallies with the Cosmo drawing; it was an imposing range, about 100 feet in width. Secondly, Walker's representation of the Clock Tower over the bakehouse range shows no clock face; there is no mention of a clock face in the accounts for 1589-90, but there was certainly a clock—in July 1590, Walter Madison, the chief estate carpenter, rode to London to fetch '3 bells for the clock'. Walker's tower shows an elevated, balustraded 'Walk'; the accounts record that Andrew Clark, a Brentwood joiner, received 6s.6d. 'for turning of 48 balusters for the walk about the new clock tower'. The accounts also state that Richard Springfield, son of the master bricklayer, was paid 2s.6d. 'for white finishing the table under the eaves of the new clock tower'; this white finish is faithfully depicted by Walker. Thirdly, the accounts for 1593-94 state that the banqueting house in the corner of the Great Garden was built of brick but was 'white finished' by Richard Springfield; it was given a slate roof (a rarity in Elizabethan times) by Edmund Sendall, hellier, of Ratcliffe. Walker's drawing is a bare $\frac{3}{16}$-inch wide, but it depicts these two features clearly. On the slate roof, John Kendall, plumber of Witham, placed five ridges of lead; Walker plainly shows a double-hipped roof—and a double-hipped roof has five ridges.

Walker's proved accuracy in his West Horndon drawings enables his drawing of another 'lost' mansion to be interpreted with assurance. This is Moulsham Hall, Chelmsford, begun in the mid-16th century by Thomas Mildmay, Auditor of the Court of Augmentations, and completed by his son, Sir Thomas Mildmay, a close friend of Sir John Petre.[11] This house was demolished, a range at a time, by Benjamin Mildmay, Earl Fitzwalker, between 1728 and c.1745; on its foundations, Fitzwalker built a handsome country house, designed by Leoni.[12] This house, in turn, was demolished in 1809.

Walker's map of Moulsham, 1591,[13] has little supporting documentary evidence. The only other pictorial representation is a drawing in La Serre's *Histoire de l'Entrée de la Reyne,* a description of Queen Marie de' Medici's visit to England in 1639. It is of very questionable value. It is not an imaginary or a conventional drawing; it bears a slight resemblance to Walker's and appears to have been drawn from an imperfect memory. Moreover, unlike Walker's drawing, it shows a moat; this is suspect, especially as Fitzwalker found some difficulty in bringing an adequate water supply to his partially completed house in 1733.[14]

Walker shows the causeway to the house bending round from what is now St. John's Road, Chelmsford, passing farm buildings and a brick dovehouse and approaching the front of an irregular gatehouse range, about 180 feet in length. The way through the gatehouse leads to a large outer court with stables on either side and two brick gateways, at the far end. A middle court, with a brick building to the left, stands in front of the main house. Farther to the left are a formal garden and an orchard with what may well be a pleached arbour in one corner (Plate VIII).

The main house is quadrangular, around an inner courtyard. It is two-storeyed throughout, with a single-storeyed range running off to the north. The main frontage, about 130 feet in width, has five gables and an off-centre arched carriageway; the other three ranges show only one gable apiece. Every building in the complex is tiled. The main house, the north range and the outer buildings are plastered. It may never be known if the plaster covered brick or timber-framing, or even some of one and some of the other, as at Ingatestone Hall (a contemporary house of much the same size), where the main block was of brick and the rest timber-framed. The odds at Moulsham are decidedly on timber-framing: Tudor gentlemen were generally too pleased with brick to wish to cover it. Moreover, the mid-16th century was a social watershed, at least in Essex: in the second half of the century brick was a *sine qua non*, an 'in' material, for the very grand. But when Thomas Mildmay, the Auditor, began to build, the remarkable Mildmays were still climbing rapidly up the social ladder. If the building had been delayed for a generation, the buildings would certainly have been built in brick as the Petres did, partly, at Ingatestone, and, wholly, at West Horndon. Keeping up with the Petres was an essential Elizabethan exercise in Essex.

The elder Walker's map of Chelmsford, 1591 (Plate V), may well be the best in existence for showing the form and structure of an Elizabethan town. It is happily in excellent condition, and every detail is clear. The parish church (now the Cathedral), flanked by New Street on the east and Duke Street on the south-west, looks over the houses along the southern end of the churchyard to the timber-framed Sessions House (where John Johnson's Georgian Shire Hall now stands) at the head of High Street. This Sessions House was a gabled canopy (with an upper room in the roof space), supported by oak posts; there the Assize judge and the Quarter Sessions justices of the peace sat literally in open court. At other times it was used by the corn merchants. Down the Middle Row in the High Street were the shops and market stalls. On either hand and along the side streets were 'more than three hundred habitations', all 'well-built for timber and tile'. Some were clearly medieval hall-houses; some were less than a century old; all had acquired chimneys. The small number of three-storeyed houses shows that craftsmen had not yet begun in earnest to build upwards, but the pressure on restricted sites had begun: wings reached by cartways (marked

		Boxted 1586 D/DEl P1	Moulsham 1591 (town part excluded) D/DM P2	W.Horndon 1598 D/DP P2	Ingatestone 1601 (village street excluded) D/DP P8	Matching 1609 D/DU 25	E.Hanningfield 1615 D/DP P10	TOTAL	%
One-storeyed cottage	THATCHED / TILED	26 / 3 → 29	15 / 11 → 26	4 / 16 → 20	13 / 16 → 29	13 / 4 → 17	12 / 26 → 38	159	61·6
Open hall and one two-storeyed crosswing	THATCHED / TILED	1 / ~ → 1	2 / 3 → 5	~ / 3 → 3	~ / 21 → 21	1 / 2 → 3	~ / 7 → 7	40	15·5
Open hall and two two-storeyed crosswings	THATCHED / TILED	~ / 2 → 2	~ / 2 → 2	~ / 3 → 3	~ / 7 → 7	~ / ~ → 0	~ / 2 → 2	16	6·6
Two-storeyed block on rectangular plan	THATCHED / TILED	~ / 3 → 3	~ / 2 → 2	~ / 2 → 2	~ / 4 → 4	1 / 1 → 2	~ / 5 → 5	18	6·9
Two-storeyed block and one two-storeyed crosswing	THATCHED / TILED	~ / ~ → 0	~ / ~ → 0	~ / 1 → 1	~ / ~ → 0	~ / ~ → 0	~ / 2 → 2	3	1·2
Two-storeyed block and two two-storeyed crosswings	THATCHED / TILED	~ / 1 → 1	~ / ~ → 0	~ / 2 → 2	~ / 2 → 2	~ / ~ → 0	~ / 2 → 2	7	2·7
L-shaped one-storeyed	THATCHED / TILED	1 / ~ → 1	~ / ~ → 0	~ / 2 → 2	~ / 1 → 1	~ / ~ → 0	~ / ~ → 0	4	1·5
Others, mainly of more complex plan and elevation	THATCHED / TILED	~ / 1 → 1	~ / 1 → 1	~ / 4 → 4	~ / 5 → 5	~ / ~ → 0	~ / 2 → 2	11	4·3

black) were built out towards the 'backsydes'; in some houses, mainly the 'many fair inns', the wings had been joined to form courtyards. Down the street, past the little conduit, the courtyard of the *Lion*, owned by Sir John Petre, stood near Henry Yevele's bridge over the Can. The town continued over the bridge into the hamlet of Moulsham. Its abrupt termination at the edge of the map is of no consequence—fortunately, Walker's map of Moulsham, 1591, still survives, in equally good condition.[15]

There is no doubt that the street profiles are reliable. Miss Grieve found them accurate when she compiled an Elizabethan street directory of Chelmsford by checking them against Walker's written survey and the manorial records and deeds.[16] But it would be unwise to deduce too much on the *structure* of the buildings. Miss Grieve found considerable difficulty through divisions and amalgamations of *sites*. She overcame this and identified the *tenements* satisfactorily; but it would be impossible to go all the way along a street distinguishing every structural unity in turn from those on either side; besides, it would be quite possible for two tenements or more to be included in any one structural unity, or even for one family to be occupying parts of two structural entities.

It is in their maps of *rural* areas that the Walkers became most valuable guides to types of vernacular architecture. An analysis of buildings on six Walker maps (p.86) shows that 61.6% of all houses were the cottages of relatively poor people. This was to be expected, but it opens up the possibility of a study which has been neglected, probably because so many people think that the structural evidence no longer exists. Even G. M. Trevelyan wrote 'the farms and cottages of the poor were built of logs or planks or of uprights and beams supporting rubble and clay . . . But since these humble homes have disappeared, we know very little about them.'[17] Undoubtedly many of them did perish, but there are more surviving than most people imagine. They are to be found heavily disguised by alterations, particularly those made during the latter half of the great period of rebuilding from *c.*1570 to *c.*1640 or even later. And they were not flimsy structures, but far more substantial than many built (not rebuilt) in the 17th century. So far about 50 early cottages are known in Essex.[18] The date range appears to be from the late 14th century to 1580. They are all 'single-storeyed', or, more accurately, of one and a half storeys. Their layout consists of three or four bays (five bays in one instance) on an unjettied, rectangular plan. Two bays (the middle two in a four-bay cottage) originally formed an open hall, as witnessed by sooted rafters and, in one house at Chrishall, a surviving open hearth. The end bay or bays were usually ceiled in by an upper floor set below tiebeam level, thus providing adequate head height on the ground floor and also utilising the roof space for the upper room. As the top wall plate and tie beams were at less than waist height in the upper rooms, the only suitable position for a window was for it to be set in the end wall over the tiebeams. Windows in this position help in the recognition of this type of house. In Elizabethan times or in the 17th century, those changes common to open medieval hall houses generally were made to these known Essex examples—chimney stacks were inserted, the hall bays were divided horizontally by intruded floors and dormer windows were built.

Naturally, a close watch was kept for an existing medieval-type cottage on the site of a Walker drawing. Doubtful examples were examined, but in all of these the main timbers were so heavily obscured by plaster and later accretions that no certain judgement could be made. Then a splendid example, Vine Cottage, was discovered at Boxted in north-east Essex. Its front elevation on Walker's survey of Rivers Hall estate, Boxted, 1586 (Plate XXXVIII) corresponds closely with a modern photograph (Plate XXXVIII); the main difference is the addition of a 17th century gable; other alterations are known to have been carried out in this present century. It was built with four bays; the main framework is original; so, too, are many of the rafters. Each top-plate has a halved and bridled scarf. The tall central crown-post in the former two-bay open hall has an unusual moulded capital; the post itself is chamfered; its base is not visible (Plate XXXVIII). The post, braces, central purlin and rafters are soot-encrusted. The main stack probably belongs to the early 16th century; it is inserted in the narrower of the hall bays. The date of the main framing is probably early 15th century. Also in Boxted is Dolf's Cottage, another 'Walker' building, dating from c.1500 (Plate XXXVII).

The diagram (p.86) shows a preponderance of thatch over tile in the cottages in the Boxted and Matching maps; on the West Horndon, Ingatestone and East Hanningfield maps it is the other way round. Too much should not be read into this. Certainly the owners of West Horndon and Ingatestone manors (Sir John Petre) and East Hanningfield (Lord Bergavenny) were prosperous magnates who kept their estates in good order; certainly, all three manors were in or very near centres of brick and tile-making. Only three cottages of the 147 recorded on the diagram are shown without a chimney stack. Nearly all the stacks were undoubtedly of brick; they are shown in typical Walker manner—in bright red, with exaggerated capping. But a few stacks are smaller in size, shown without capping and coloured a yellowish brown. The most striking of these are not shown in cottages but, most curiously, in two brick kilns in Potter Row, Ingatestone (Plate XVI). It is possible that these small stacks could be the outlets for timbered smoke hoods.

Next in number to cottages on the diagram are open-hall houses with one two-storeyed crosswing. This vindicates the opinion, long held by the authors, that only large and important medieval hall-houses in Essex (e.g. Baythorn Hall, Birdbrook) had two original or very early crosswings— a service wing and a solar wing. *The Royal Commission on Historical Monuments,* Essex (4 vols.), frequently states that a hall-house had two crosswings, but one had been destroyed; the fact is that the many surviving Essex medieval hall-houses had only one original crosswing, with buttery and pantry on the ground floor and private rooms above. Where two crosswings now exist, the second wing was added during the rebuilding period of late Elizabethan and early Stuart times. This feature is now generally recognised. Indeed, the 15.5% shown on the diagram is almost certainly an underestimate: a number of this type may well be 'embedded' in the percentages for types 3, 5 and 6; in fact, the raising of hall roofs, the horizontal division of open halls and the addition of wings are well-known building changes, noted at least as far back as the publication of the Royal Commission's volumes for Essex, 1916-23.

The only other type on the diagram which calls for comment is the two-storeyed block on a rectangular plan. The Walkers always show a horizontal line between the two storeys, but it cannot be assumed that this always represents front-jettying although in many examples this was undoubtedly so. Examples from the 14th century are known, but in Essex it became fashionable during the third quarter of the 15th century and continued until the early 17th century or later; indeed, Cecil Hewett has discovered one or two examples of post-1650.[19] It is a compact, satisfactory type, easily adapted to changing modes of living. It could be argued that it is superior constructionally to the normal hall-house or its 'Wealden' equivalent; certainly it is a type which can easily be turned into a 'highly desirable residence' well-suited to modern living. Incidentally, Walker maps do not record a single 'Wealden' house. These are about thirty known examples in the county, and a few more may be discovered.

An attempt is being made to use the Walkers' drawings as a statistical basis for estimating the number of vernacular buildings in Essex which contain medieval elements. In 1923, the Royal Commission stated that these were 'some 750 buildings of a date anterior to the Reformation'.[20] Some of these have since disappeared, but even from casual observation it is obvious that the Commission considerably underestimated the number. Those Commissioners and investigators of sixty years ago, an understaffed and underfinanced body of eminent scholars, should not be blamed. They worked under difficulties, against time and without the considerable corpus of knowledge of timber-framed structures which has been accumulated in recent years.

The method used has been to take a Walker map and note how many secular buildings on it are recorded as medieval by the Royal Commission.

Then the map has been compared with the Ordnance Survey and a note made of present buildings which are on Walker sites. Then a reconnaissance has been made of these present buildings to judge how many might be worth close attention. So far, reconnaissance has shown that many Walker buildings no longer survive and that some existing buildings are patently post-Walker rebuildings. Then, with the permission of the owners (refused only once) the remaining buildings on Walker sites have been carefully examined by a group of persons including Cecil Hewett and the two authors of this book.[21] So far, five group field days have been undertaken, covering $3\frac{3}{4}$ Walker maps. At the conclusion of each field day, a report has been drawn up by one member, checked and amended in draft by one or two others, and then typed and duplicated. Copies have then been sent to all owners and group members.

The result so far has been interesting. Working on the equation

$$\frac{\text{Number of medieval secular buildings newly discovered on field days + number recorded by the Royal Commission}}{\text{Number recorded by the Commission}} \times 750 = \text{Possible number of medieval secular buildings remaining in Essex,}$$

the total is 4,500. Obviously the whole exercise is open to a good deal of criticism. The number of field days undertaken has been small, and even if all the Essex Walker maps had been covered, this would represent only a small part of the county (see distribution map, p.12). In other parts of the county, ancient buildings may never have been as plentiful. In some parts the destruction may have been much greater; in the extreme south-west of the ancient geographical county, for instance, very little has survived the remorseless advance of London. On the other hand, very many hitherto unrecorded old buildings are being discovered by Cecil Hewett and Adrian Gibson, and by that admirable team, the Historic Buildings and Conservation Section of the Essex County Planning Department. In short there are far too many imponderables, but at least the exercise goes some way to confirm an opinion formed from wider but more casual observations—that it would be difficult to match elsewhere the heritage of medieval timber-framing in Essex and the adjacent areas of east Hertfordshire and south Suffolk. The only possible rival is Kent.

These group field days on Walker map areas, as well as visits by only two or three persons at a time, have convinced those concerned that, ideally, every house on a Walker site ought to be closely investigated. Occasionally, the house on the site is obviously the one shown by the Walkers, with virtually little alteration. Sometimes part of a Walker house survives and can be immediately recognized. Sometimes, the alterations are so extensive that only close examination reveals parts of the house depicted by Walker. Quite apart from buildings in Ingatestone village street, the great

THE WALKERS OF HANNINGFIELD

Ingatestone map of 1601 shows at least 18 examples which belong to one or another of these three categories. The colours on the Little Hyde area of the map have shelled slightly (Plate XXXVI (a)); even so it is quite easy to make out a typical open hall-house with two crosswings and a long building of irregular shape. Today, the long building has a cladding of 18th century brick and a modern crosswing (Plate XXXVI (c)); inside, most of the structure is covered over, but sufficient remains exposed to show that the main block is timber-framed and its rafters, set flat, are soot-covered. The hall-house has scarcely changed (Plate XXXVI (b)). Less than a mile away are Harding's Farm (formerly, Haldins), Murcockes and Redindyke. Harding's Farm (Plate XXXVII) is obviously just half of the house shown on Walker, sliced right down the middle of the hall (Plate XXXVII). John Walker junior shows Murcockes as a timbered, open hall-house with one crosswing (Plate XXXVI (f)). The present building (Plate XXXVI (g)) is described in the Department of the Environment list as a brick building of the 18th century, though the irregularity of the fenestration and the survival of one late 16th century stack should have alerted the Ministry's investigators to its greater age. The brick is merely a $4\frac{1}{2}$-inch skin and although 18th-century alterations have obscured or destroyed much of the earlier work, part of the original timbering of the crosswing survives, and there are 18 couples of soot-encrusted reused rafters, obviously from a collar-purlin, crown-post roof over the former hall. Walker shows 'Ridden Dyke' as an extremely complicated timber-framed house (Plate XXXVI (d)); the present Redindyke (Plate XXXVI (e)) is merely one of the former crosswings. It stands, incidentally, on one of those rarely-recorded medieval enclosures from forest land; among the Petre archives is a charter of c.1225[22] by which the abbess and convent of Barking confirmed to their steward, John de Geyton, an assart or clearance—'ridden' of the trees and scrub—which they had made. This may help to date the oldest parts of the house shown by Walker.

It would be easy to multiply examples from the Ingatestone map, but it is more profitable to turn to the map of Housham Hall, Matching, 1609, also drawn by the younger Walker, because, here, most of the buildings are grouped in three compact areas. The first of these shows Housham Hall itself and is obviously an important site (Plate XVIII (a)). Apart from changes in buildings, there is a close similarity between Walker's map and the 25-inch O.S. map, and between these and the position today: the house and farm buildings are attractively grouped; to their north-west is a moated enclosure (the moat, complete on Walker and the O.S., was being steadily filled in when the site was first visited in 1962); to the south of the enclosure and west of the buildings is a small meadow, called the 'Foreburie' by Walker, though this name has now been transfered to a field immediately east of the farmhouse. Incidentally, even Walker nodded occasionally!—he does not mark the site of the chapel in the 'Foreburie', although its ruins existed in Morant's time and the site is marked in the 25-inch O.S. map.[23] Walker shows the following buildings, all timber-framed; a late medieval open hall-house, with two-storeyed crosswing, a thatched roof and a brick chimney stack in or near the screens passage; two thatched barns, one of them large; a thatched open cart shed; a small, tiled building, probably a stable; another fairly large, tiled building; a thatched building with two entries, possibly an oxhouse. Of these, the following survive, wholly or in part:

(i)   Part of the house. The Ministry of Housing and Local Government list (1960) does not mention this. There was, as the M.H.L.G. list indicates, a thorough remodelling of the house in the 18th century (Plate XXXIX), but the northern part is undoubtedly the late medieval crosswing shown by Walker, but with a Georgian roof.

(ii)   The smaller barn is probably much as it was in Walker's time, when it may have been fairly new (Plate XXXIX).

(iii)   The larger barn is the building shown by Walker. It is aisled, and possibly medieval in date (Plate XXXIX).

The second settlement is Housham Tye, formerly the main settlement of manorial tenants around a common (Plate XVIII (b)). In Walker's time, most of the buildings were single-storeyed cottages; today only two or three of these structures survive. The smaller thatched cottage against the top left-hand corner of the common has been much altered, but the framework of its western end may be original. On the site of the only tiled open hall-house with one crosswing, a fairly large house now stands (Plate XXXIX). The Ministry list describes it as 'of 17th-century origin but greatly added to and modernised'. There is nothing showing externally to question in this statement, but inside is a good deal of medieval framing *in situ,* as well as reused medieval timbers.

The third Housham area is the hamlet of Newlands End, now called Newman's End (Plate XVIII (c)). Walker shows a mixed collection of buildings facing in various directions—as mentioned earlier, the Walkers always give the true base line. Perhaps the most interesting are a thatched open cartshed, the parson's tiled tithe barn and his tiled granary perched on brick piers. Only two, possibly three, buildings survive: the two-storeyed, late medieval house near the base of the map, the thatched cottage to the right of the word 'Newlandes', and one of the two buildings called 'Personage Howse'. This parsonage cottage was rebuilt in the 17th century and altered in Georgian times, but a number of medieval timbers were reused.

The Chronological Catalogue describes, *inter alia,* the present condition of all Walker maps. Perhaps the one nearest to mint condition is the younger Walker's Mascallsbury in the parish of White Roothing, 1609. The area of Mascallsbury itself (Plate XIX) shows a settlement which bears all the marks of antiquity: a forecourt with three barns, and open cartshed and two other buildings, all thatched; a moated site, entered through a gatehouse; within, two outbuildings, one probably a kitchen,[24] and the main building itself, partly a late medieval open hall-house with one crosswing and partly Elizabethan. Walker even shows two thatched dog kennels. Part of an existing barn may be part of one of the barns depicted by Walker; otherwise, all his outbuildings have disappeared. Part of the moat is still there; so, too, is most of the house; a Regency block has been added at one end and the rest has been given a Regency façade.

In this chapter, the emphasis has been on the value of Walker drawings to the study of building *structures*. There is, however, another important way in which they can be used: in conjunction with other documentary evidence they can form a starting-point for a detailed historical study of a town, village or rural area—a starting point for the simple reason that they are the only reliable *visual* evidence of early date. As indicated earlier, Miss Hilda Grieve found the elder Walker's map of Chelmsford, 1591, an absolutely reliable starting-point for her (still unfinished) history of Chelmsford. In the Introduction it is mentioned that one of the authors of this book used the map of Ingatestone, 1601, for a tentative experiment in compiling a village history. It happens that the village street of Ingatestone, formerly part of the modern A12 (now bypassed) from London to Colchester, lies on the boundary of the manors of Ingatestone and Fryerning. Walker shows the buildings on both sides of the street, but only the south-east side from Stock Lane to the *Crown* (Plate XV) is in the manor of Ingatestone. This section is remarkably well documented. There is a written survey of 1602,[25] not in the handwriting of either of the Walkers but intended to go with their map. There is also an earlier survey of *c.* 1556,[26] which gives the dimensions of the buildings including height to the eaves. Using the map and these surveys and the evidence of the court rolls, it was found possible to build up a fairly complete record of that part of the street throughout the reign of Queen Elizabeth I—the map and surveys provided the names of occupants and the kind of houses they lived in, while the court rolls yielded information on the lives of the occupants. The choice of the Elizabethan period for this experiment was fortuitous, but it happens to cover the first half of the greatest period of rebuilding, *c.* 1570-*c.* 1640, first pointed out by Professor Hoskins. Certainly there was considerable rebuilding along that stretch of street: in 1556 there were 15 single-storeyed cottages; by 1601, nine of them had become two-storeyed. This limited study could be extended forwards into this century and backwards to 1279, as the court rolls and court books form a virtually complete series. There is a good deal of additional original evidence, including medieval documents pre-dating the earliest court rolls. The point about work of this kind is that where there is no reliable early map, the researcher, sooner or later has to evolve one with great labour. The Walkers provide invaluable, ready-made visual certainty at an early date.

Perhaps a cautionary tale should be added. The other author of this book noticed that there were ancient buildings surviving on only two of the sites where single-storeyed cottages in 1556 had become two-storeyed by 1601. Both buildings were front-jettied, and he wondered if the second storey had been just put on, like a hat. This would have raised interesting speculation on methods of construction. Alas, when one of these buildings was being stripped and demolished in November, 1964, it was found that there had been a complete rebuilding between 1556 and 1601 exactly on the medieval site. The other building was carefully examined in October, 1965, and found to be a rebuilding from the ground upwards. These tiny Walker drawings yield remarkable evidence; they should not be used as a basis for unwarranted speculation. Good friends should be treated with gratitude and consideration!

Notes and References
Unless stated otherwise, all catalogue marks refer to documents in the Essex Record Office.

1. *The Map of Mid-Sixteenth Century London,* London Topographical Society, 1964.
2. Licence to Lewis John, 1414, to embattle West Horndon Hall, D/DP T1/181. See also, A. D. Carr: 'Sir Lewis John—A Medieval London Welshman', in the *Bulletin of the Board of Celtic Studies,* Vol. 22, Part 3, 1967.
3. See *Old Thorndon Hall* (E.R.O. Pubn. No. 61, 1972). This consists of an account by Dr. Jennifer Ward of the Elizabethan rebuilding and the Report on the excavations at Old Thorndon Hall, 1957-59, by the late Kenneth Marshall, edited by Ian Robertson.
4. D/DP T135/86.
5. Petre account books, D/DP A18-22. See also, *John Petre,* Chapter 5, by A. C. Edwards.
6. D/DP P5.
7. D/DP P145A, B.
8. D/DP P23/1.
9. D/DP A21.
10. D/DP A22.

11. Morant: *History of Essex,* II, 3. Morant quotes from Walker's written survey of Moulsham, 1591, now lost.

12. For the Georgian rebuilding of Moulsham Hall, see Fitzwalter account books, D/DM A5-7, and D/DMy 15M50/31. Leoni's plan is reproduced in *Vitruvius Britannicus,* Plate 30. A full narrative of this rebuilding is given in *The Account Books of Benjamin Mildmay, Earl Fitzwalter,* pp.28-64, by A. C. Edwards.

13. D/DM P2.

14. D/DM A5.

15. Much of the information in this paragraph is derived from Walker's written survey of Chelmsford, 1591, D/DGe M50.

16. During her research, Miss Grieve has compiled maps of Chelmsford for 1086, 1086-1381, 1381, 1461-1509, 1591, 1676, 1787 and 1888. Those from 1381 onwards are accompanied by detailed street directories and fascinating side lights on the lives of Chelmsford citizens.

17. *Illustrated English Social History,* I, 19-20.

18. See A. V. B. Gibson, 'Some small unjettied medieval houses in Essex', *Essex Journal,* Spring, 1974.

19. *Medieval Archaeology,* X, 1966, 104.

20. *Royal Commission on Historical Monuments (Essex),* IV, xxxv.

21. It was agreed that most of this work should be carried out by a group on the principle that several pairs of eyes are better than two—and more likely to be believed by sceptics! This has necessarily limited the number of full scale field days which could be organised and undertaken, and has entailed the exclusion of some buildings which, although old, seemed from inspection of their exteriors to be so much altered that the discovery of medieval elements was unlikely.

22. D/DP T1/653.

23. Morant: *History of Essex,* II, 499. John McCann, who read this chapter, rightly commented that the Walkers were 'not archaeologists surveying ruins, but surveyors recording the current assets of the landed proprietors who were their clients'.

24. It is almost impossible to identify medieval kitchens on Walker maps. Medieval court rolls make it clear that kitchens belonging to vernacular houses were detached or semi-detached; they are listed with stables and other outbuildings (e.g. D/DP M54); and there is no reason to suppose that they were different in shape from ordinary cottages. But a small, single-storeyed building with a chimney could be a kitchen, or it could be another cottage or a brewhouse. As to larger, tall, detached timber-framed kitchens, belonging to more important houses and being roughly equivalent to medieval stone

kitchens, such as the Abbot's kitchen, Glastonbury, there is an obvious example shown on a Walker map. This was at Springfield Hall in the Springfield map of c.1616 (Plate XXVIII). The house survives, but much altered in Georgian and later times; a square building at the back may have been built on the foundations of the kitchen. There is another possible example in the Chelmsford map, 1591 (Plate V). An actual timber-framed kitchen, not on a Walker site, exists at Little Braxted Hall. *The Royal Commission on Historical Monuments (Essex),* III, 163, describes it as a barn(!), and then says that it 'may possibly have been the hall of the former house'! It is fairly tall, square in plan, and is lit or ventilated high up by tall windows, each divided by one thick mullion set diamondwise. The roof is supported by a sooted arched truss; at the apex, where the louvre would have been, are more modern timbers, indicating considerable alteration. The date is probably late 14th century or *c.*1400. See C. A. Hewett, 'A medieval timber kitchen at Little Braxted,' *Medieval Archaeology,* 17, 1973, pp.132-4.

25. D/DP M1449.
26. D/DP M170.

Diagrammatic analyses
of buildings on
ten Walker maps

Type of Building	Variation of features with number of examples thus (-)	Total
A. One-storeyed cottages 1. With thatched roof and wooden smoke-hood.	 (1) (1) (1) (1) (1)	5
2. With thatched roof and brick chimney.	 (1) (1) (1) (1) (3) (2) (1) (2) (1) (2) (1) (1) (1)	18
3. As 2., L-plan.	 (1)	1
4. As 2., 'semi-detached'.	 (1)	1
5. With thatched roof and no chimney or smoke-hood.	 (2)	2
6. With tiled roof and brick chimney.	 (1) (1) (1)	3
B. Open hall with crosswing(s) 1. With one two-storeyed crosswing, thatched roofs and brick chimneys.	 (1)	1
2. With one two-storeyed crosswing at either end, tiled roofs and brick chimney.	 (2)	2
3. As 2., with additions to form courtyard-type house.	 (1)	1
C. Two-storeyed houses 1. Simple elevation, tiled roof and brick chimney.	 (1) (1) (1)	3
2. With two-storeyed crosswing at either end, tiled roofs and brick chimney.	 (1)	1
D. Other buildings 1. Churches	Boxted church [See Plate III; also Catalogue, p. 43]	1
2. Barns thatched	 (17) (4) (1) (1)	23
3. Other outbuildings thatched	 (3) (1) (1) (2)	7

CHELMSFORD, 1591

Analysis of Buildings (in rural area only; for town area, see Plate V)   **TABLE 2**

Type of Building	Variation of features with number of examples thus (-)	Total
A. One-storeyed cottages 1. With thatched roof and wooden smoke-hood.	(1) (1) (1) (1) (1)	5
2. With thatched roof and brick chimney.	(1) (1) (1) (1)	4
3. With thatched roof and no chimney or smoke-hood.	(1)	1
4. As 2, 'semi-detached'.	(1)	1
5. With tiled roof and brick chimney.	(1)	1
B. Two-storeyed houses Four bays, tiled roofs, brick chimneys.	(1)	1
C. Range of two and one-storeyed dwellings and outbuildings Tiled roofs and brick chimneys.	(1)	1
D. Other buildings 1. Watermill, tiled roof and brick chimney.	(1)	1
2. Barns (a) thatched	(1) (1)	2
(b) tiled	(2)	2
3. Other outbuildings (a) thatched	(1) (1)	2
(b) tiled	(1)	1

Type of Building	Variation of features with number of examples thus (-)	Total
A. One-storeyed cottages 1. With thatched roof and wooden smoke-hood.		11
2. As 1., 'semi-detached'.		1
3. With thatched roof and brick chimney.		3
4. With tiled roof and brick chimney.		9
5. As 4., 'semi-detached'.		2
B. Open hall with crosswing(s) 1. With one two-storeyed crosswing, thatched roofs and brick chimney.		1
2. With one two-storeyed tiled crosswing, thatched hall and brick chimney.		1
3. With one two-storeyed crosswing, tiled roofs and brick chimney.		3
4. With one two-storeyed crosswing at either end, tiled roofs and brick chimney.		2
C. Two-storeyed houses Simple elevation, tiled roof and brick chimney.		2
D. Houses of more complex elevation	Moulsham Hall [See Plate VIII]	1
E. Other buildings 1. Churches	Widford Church [See Plate VIII]	1
2. Watermills, with tiled roof and brick chimney.		1
3. Barns (a) thatched		9
(b) tiled		2
4. Detached kitchen or brewhouse(?)		1
5. Other outbuildings (a) thatched		3
(b) tiled		3
	Notes * The smoke-hoods on these cottages appear to have been intentionally exaggerated more than usual. † The chimney of this cottage has been similarly treated.	

Type of Building	Variation of features with number of examples thus (-)	Total
A. One-storeyed cottages 1. With thatched roof and wooden smoke-hood.	(5)　(1)　(3)　(4)　(1)　(1)　(1)　(1)　(1)	18
2. With thatched roof and brick chimney.	(1)　(1)*　(1)*　(1)　(1)　(1)	6
3. With tiled roof and brick chimney.	(1)†　(1)　(1)　(1)　(1)　(1)	6
4. With thatched roof and no chimney or smoke-hood.	(1)　(1)†	2
B. Open hall with crosswing With one two-storeyed crosswing, tiled roofs and brick chimney(s).	(1)　(1)　(1)　(1)	4
C. Two-storeyed houses with crosswings 1. With one two-storeyed crosswing at either end, tiled roofs and brick chimneys.	(1)	1
2. As 1., L-plan.	(1)	1
D. Two-storeyed houses, simple elevation Tiled roof and brick chimney.	(1)　(1)	2
E. Other buildings 1. Churches	Terling Church [See Plate IX]	1
2. Barns (a) thatched	(2)　(1)　(1)	4
(b) tiled	(1)	1
3. Other outbuildings (a) thatched	(1)　(1)　(1)　(1)	4
(b) tiled	(1)　(1)　(1)**　(1)††	4
	Notes *　The chimney on this cottage is uncoloured, but it is assumed that this is an oversight, rather than an attempt to show a different building material. †　Other features indistinguishable. **　A banqueting house. ††　A brick and tile building, purpose unknown.	

Type of Building	Variation of features with number of examples thus (-)	Total
A. One-storeyed cottages		
1. With thatched roof and wooden smoke-hood.	(1) (1) (1) *	3
2. With thatched roof and brick chimney.	(1)	1
3. With tiled roof and brick chimney.	(2) (1) (2) (1) (1) (1) (3) (2) (1) (1)	15
4. As 3., with single storeyed extension.	(1)	1
5. As 3., L-plan	(1) (1)	2
B. Open hall with crosswing(s)		
1. With one two-storeyed crosswing, tiled roofs and brick chimney.	(1) (1) (1)	3
2. With one two-storeyed crosswing at either end, tiled roofs and brick chimney.	(1) (1) (1)	3
C. Two-storeyed houses		
1. Simple elevation, tiled roof and brick chimneys.	(1)	1
2. As 1., with two-storeyed extension.	(1)	1
3. L-plan, tiled roofs and brick chimneys.	(1)	1
4. As 3., but one wing single storeyed.	(1)	1
5. As 1., with one two-storeyed crosswing.	(1)	1
6. As 1., with one two-storeyed crosswing at either end.	(1) (1)	2
D. Houses of more complex elevation.	[Old] Thorndon Hall [See Plate X] East Horndon Manor House [See Plate XI]	2

TABLE 5 cont.

Type of Building	Variation of features with number of examples thus (-)	Total
E. *Other buildings* 1. Windmills.	(1)	1
2. Churches.	West Horndon Church [See Plate X] East Horndon Church [See Plate XI]	2
3. Barns (a) thatched	(6)	6
(b) tiled	(4)　　(1)　　(1)	6
4. (?) Detached kitchens or brewhouses with tiled roof and brick chimney.†	(1)　　(1)	2
5. Other outbuildings [see also Plate X] (a) thatched	(1)　(1)　(2)　　(1)　　**	5
(b) tiled	(1)　(2)　(1)　(1)　(1)　(1)	7

Notes
* Other features of this cottage are missing through shelling of map.
† Each in close proximity to rear of house.
** Wall of brick construction.

Analysis of Buildings (excluding the 'Towne' area, for which see Plate XV)

TABLE 6

Type of Building	Variation of features with number of examples thus (-)	Total
A. *One-storeyed cottages*		
1. With thatched roof and wooden smoke-hood.	(1) (1) (1) (1)	4
2. With thatched roof and brick chimney.	(2) (3) (4)	9
3. With tiled roof and brick chimney.	(3) (3) (1) (1) (2) (4) (1)	15
4. L-plan, with tiled roofs, brick chimneys and gable windows.	(1)	1
5. As 3., with thatched outbuilding attached.	(1)	1
6. With roof part tiled and part thatched, brick chimney.	(1)	1
B. *Open hall with crosswing(s)*		
1. With one two-storeyed crosswing, tiled roofs and brick chimney(s).	(1) (1) (3) (2) (1) (1) (1) (5) (1) (1) (1) (1) (1)	20
2. As 1., with single storeyed extension against crosswing.	(1)	1
3. With one one-storeyed and one two-storeyed crosswing, tiled roofs and brick chimneys.	(1)	1
4. With one two-storeyed crossing at either end.	(2) (1) (2) (1) (1)	7

TABLE 6 cont.

Type of Building	Variation of features with number of examples thus (-)	Total
C. *Two-storeyed houses* 1. Simple elevation, tiled roof and brick chimney(s).	(1) (1) (1) (1)	4
2. L-plan, tiled roofs and brick chimneys.	(1)	1
3. Of 5 bays, tiled roofs and brick chimneys.	(1) †	1
D. *Houses of more complex elevation* Tiled roofs and brick chimneys.	(1)	1
E. *Other buildings*★★ 1. Churches††	(1) ★★★	1
2. Barns (a) thatched	(23) (1)	24
(b) tiled	(16) (1) (1) (1) (1) (1) (1)	22
3. (?) Detached kitchens or brewhouses, tiled roof, one with smoke-hood, two with brick chimney.†††	(1) (1) (1)	3
4. Other outbuildings (a) thatched	(6) (2) (5) (6) (1) (5) (1)	26
(b) tiled	(1) (5) (1) (1) (8) (1) (1) (1) (1) (1)	21
5. Dovecote, tiled.	(1)	1

Notes

★   *Unusually, one such house is shown in perspective as indicated by dotted lines.*
†   *Unusually, drawn in perspective.*
★★   *For Ingatestone windmill, see Plate XVI.*
††   *For Ingatestone Church, see Plate XV.*
★★★   *Fryerning Church. The map has unfortunately shelled a little at this point and more detail may have originally been shown than is redrawn here. The relative lengths of chancel, nave and tower accord reasonably well with those given in R.C.H.M. Essex, ii, 138; the porch is shown in the right position and the tower is correctly represented as buttressed and embattled; the doorway is now more central 'but may have been reset in the 17th century' (R.C.H.M.). The thatched roof of the nave is otherwise unrecorded.*
††† *Each situated in close proximity to rear of a house.*

Type of Building	Variation of features with number of examples thus (-)	Total
A. *One-storeyed cottages* 1. With thatched roof and no chimney or smoke-hood.	(1)	1
2. With thatched roof and brick chimney.	(1) (3) (2)	6
3. With tiled roof and brick chimney.	(1)	1
B. *Open hall with crosswing(s)* 1. With one two-storeyed crosswing, tiled roofs and brick chimney(s).	(1) (1) (1)	3
2. With one two-storeyed crosswing, at either end, tiled roofs and brick chimney.	(1) (1) (1)	3
C. *Two-storeyed houses* 1. Simple elevation, tiled roof and brick chimney.	(1) (1)	2
2. With two-storeyed crosswings at either end, tiled roofs and brick chimneys.	(1)	1
3. With three-storeyed crosswings at either end, central porch wing, tiled roofs and brick chimneys.	(1)	1
4. With central gabled wing, tiled roofs and brick chimneys.	(1)	1
D. *Buildings of more complex elevation.*	[Ingatestone Hall (see Plate XVII)]	1

TABLE 7 cont.

Type of Building	Variation of features with number of examples thus (-)	Total
E. *Other buildings* 1. Churches	(Buttsbury Church) [For Ingatestone Church, see Plate XV]	1
2. Barns (a) thatched	(7) (1)	8
(b) tiled	(1)	1
3. Other outbuildings (a) thatched	(2) (1) (3) (1)	7
(b) tiled	(2) (1) (1) (1)	5
4. Detached kitchens or brewhouses(?), thatched roof, wooden smoke-hood.	(1) (1)	2
5. Gatehouse (to moated house), tiled roof.	(1)	1

Type of Building	Variation of features with number of examples thus (-)	Total
A. One-storeyed cottages		
1. With thatched roof and wooden smoke-hood.	(1)	1
2. With thatched roof and brick chimney.	(3) (2) (1) (2) (2)	10
3. As 2., with additional wing.	(1)	1
4. With tiled roof and brick chimney(s).	(7) (1) (1) (1) (3) (2) (1) (1) (1)	18
5. As 4., with dormer windows.	(1)	1
6. As 5., with addition of a smoke-hood.	(1)	1
7. As 4., 'semi-detached'.	(1) (1) (1)	3
8. As 4., with thatched addition.	(1) (1)	2
9. With tiled roof and wooden smoke-hood.	(1)	1
B. Open hall with crosswing(s)		
1. With one two-storeyed crosswing, tiled roofs and brick chimney(s).	(1) (1) (2) (1) (1) (1)	7
2. With one two-storeyed crosswing at either end, tiled roofs, brick chimney.	(1)	1
3. As 2., with dormer window in hall roof.	(1)	1

TABLE 8 cont.

Type of Building	Variation of features with number of examples thus (-)	Total
C. Two-storeyed houses 1. With simple elevation, tiled roof and brick chimney(s).	(1) (1) (1) (1)	4
2. As 1., with one-storeyed addition.	(1)	1
3. With one two-storeyed crosswing, tiled roofs and brick chimney(s).	(1) (1)	2
4. With one two-storeyed crosswing at either end, tiled roofs and brick chimney.	(1)	1
5. As 4., with single-storeyed addition.	(1)	1
D. Houses of more complex elevation With tiled roofs and brick chimneys.	(1) (1)	2
E. Other buildings 1. Churches	[For East Hanningfield and West Hanningfield churches, see Plate XXV]	2
2. Barns (a) thatched	(3) (1)	4
(b) tiled	(18) (1) (1) (1) (1)	22
3. (?) Detached kitchen or brewhouse†, with tiled roof and smoke-hood.	(1)	1
4. Gatehouses.	(1)	1
5. Other outbuildings (a) thatched	(7) (1) (1)	9
(b) tiled	(3) (2) (1) (1) (1) (1) (1)	10

	Notes
	  * *Twin-shafted chimney(s) clearly represented on original map.*
	  † *In close proximity to rear of house.*	

Type of Building	Variation of features with number of examples thus (-)	Total
A. One-storeyed cottages		
1. With thatched roof and brick chimney.	(1)	1
2. With tiled roof and brick chimney.	(1) (3) (1) * (1) (2) (1) (6) † (1) † (1) **	17
3. As 2., L-plan.	(1)	1
4. As 2., 'terrace' type, brick walls.	(1)	1
B. Open hall with crosswing(s)		
1. With one two-storeyed crosswing, tiled roofs and brick chimney.	(2) (1)	3
2. With one two-storeyed crosswing at either end, tiled roofs and brick chimney(s).	(2) (1) (1) (1) *	5
C. Two-storeyed houses		
1. Simple elevation, tiled roof and brick chimney.	(1) *	1
2. With one two-storeyed crosswing, tiled roofs and brick chimney.	(1)	1
3. With one two-storeyed crosswing at either end, tiled roofs and brick chimney.	(1) *	1
D. Other buildings		
1. Churches.	[For Buttsbury and Stock churches, see Plate XXVII]	2
2. Barns, tiled.	(4) (1)	5
3. Other outbuildings.	(1) (3) (1)	5
	Notes * Twin-shafted chimney clearly represented on original map. † Other features of these cottages now illegible on original map. ** Dormer window in roof.	

Type of Building	Variation of features with number of examples thus (-)	Total
A. Single-storeyed cottages With tiled roof and brick chimney.	(1) (12) (1) (1) (1) (1) (4) (1) (7)*	29
B. Open hall with crosswing(s) 1. With one two-storeyed crosswing, tiled roofs and brick chimney.	(1) (1) (1)	3
2. With one two-storeyed crosswing at either end, tiled roofs and brick chimney(s).	(2) (3) (1)	6
C. Two-storeyed houses 1. With simple elevation, tiled roof and brick chimney.	(3) (1)† (1)† (1) (1)** (1)**	8
2. With one two-storeyed crosswing, tiled roofs and brick chimney(s).	(1) (1)	2
3. With one two-storeyed crosswing at either end, tiled roof and brick chimneys.	(2) (1)	3
D. Houses of more complex elevation Tiled roofs and brick chimney(s).	(1) (1)	2
E. Other buildings 1. Churches.	[For Springfield Church, see Plate XXIX]	1
2. Barns, tiled.	(6)	6
3. As 2., but part of a range.	(1)	1
4. (?) Detached kitchens or brewhouses, tiled roof and brick chimney.††	(2)	2
5. Other outbuildings, tiled.	(1) (2) (1) (1)*** (1) (1)††† (1)	8

	Notes
	  * Other features of these cottages now illegible on original map.
	  † Twin-shafted chimney clearly represented on original map.
	  ** Dotted lines represent parts of buildings obscured by drawings of others.
	  †† Each located in close proximity to rear of house.
	  *** Open cart-shed.
	  ††† A medieval kitchen.	

The Walker Maps

List of Illustrations

PLATE I

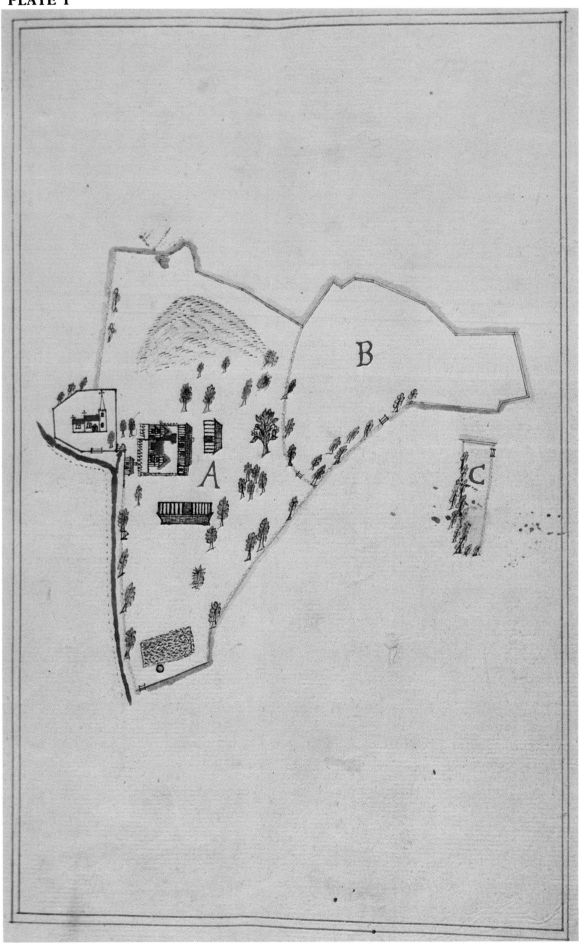

Map of West Tilbury Hall, 1584.

PLATE II

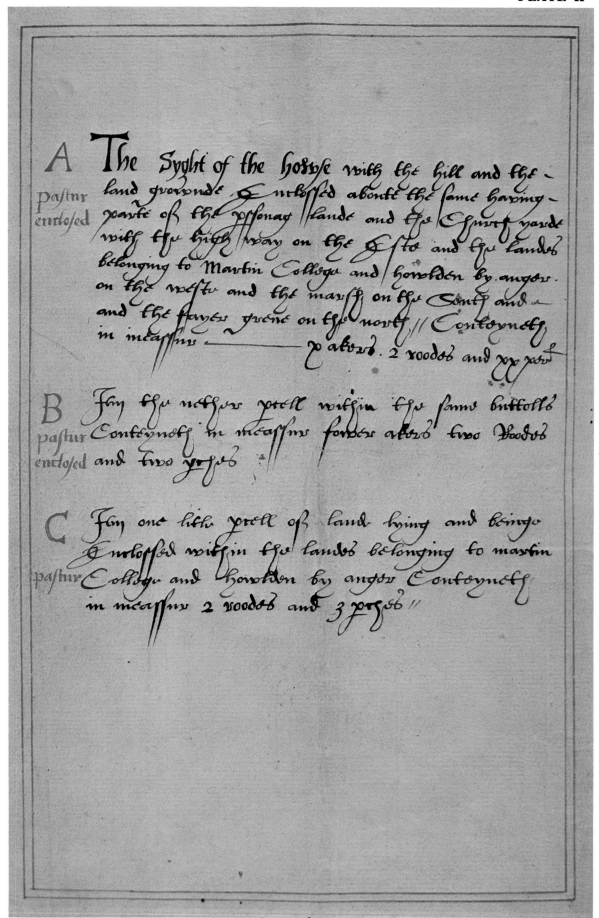

A pastur entlofed

The Syght of the howse with the hill and the land growde Enclosed abowte the same having parte off the personay landes and the Church yarde with the high way on the Este and the landes belonging to Martin Colldge and howlden by angow on the weste and the marssh on the South and and the fayers grene on the north // Contoyneth in meassur ———— p akers. 2 roodes and xx perch

B pastur entlofed

For the nether prell within the same buttolls Contoyneth in meassur fowre akers two roodes and two yrdes

C pastur

For one litle prell off land lying and beinge Enclosed within the landes belonging to martin Colldge and howlden by angow Contoyneth in meassur 2 roodes and 3 prches //

Description of West Tilbury Hall, 1584.

PLATE III

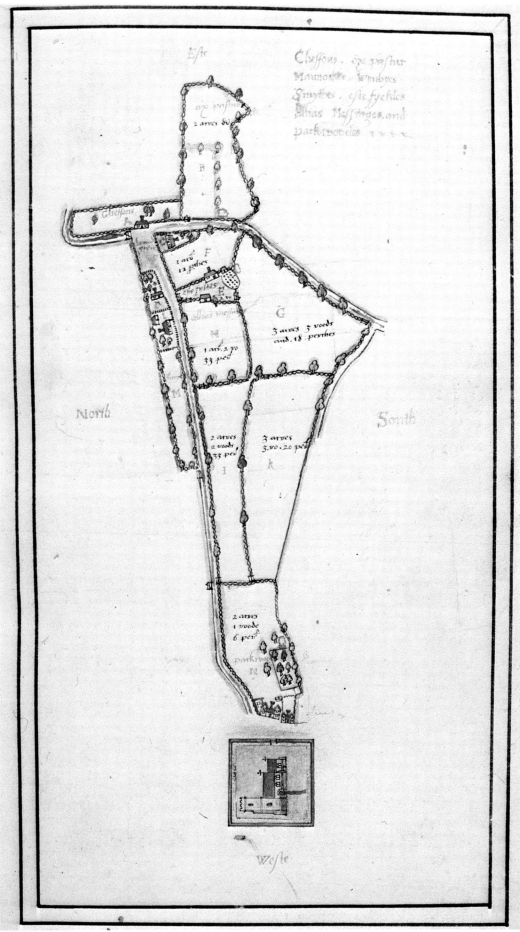

From the survey of Boxted, 1586 (slightly enlarged).

PLATE IV

From the survey of the
Manor of Mowden
Hall in Hatfield
Peverel, 1589.

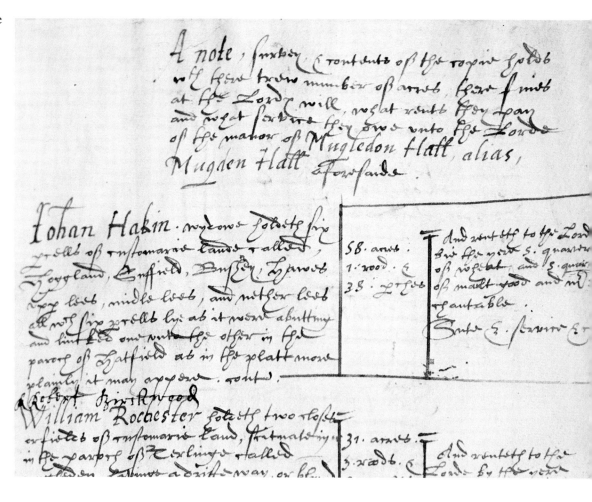

A small farm at Broomfield, 1591.

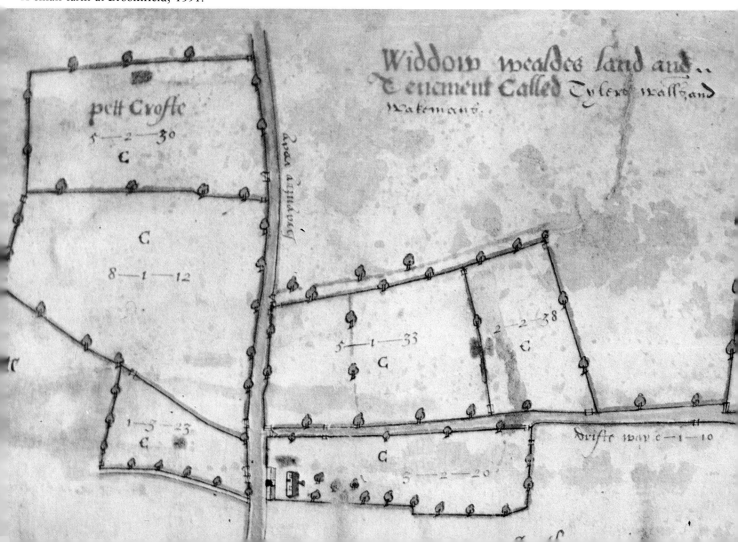

PLATE V

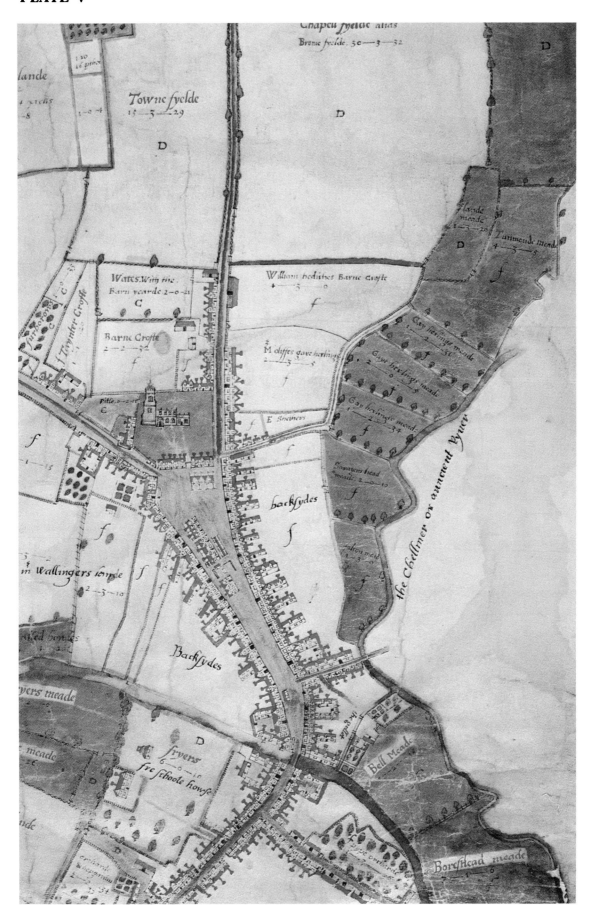

Chelmsford in 1591 (slightly reduced).

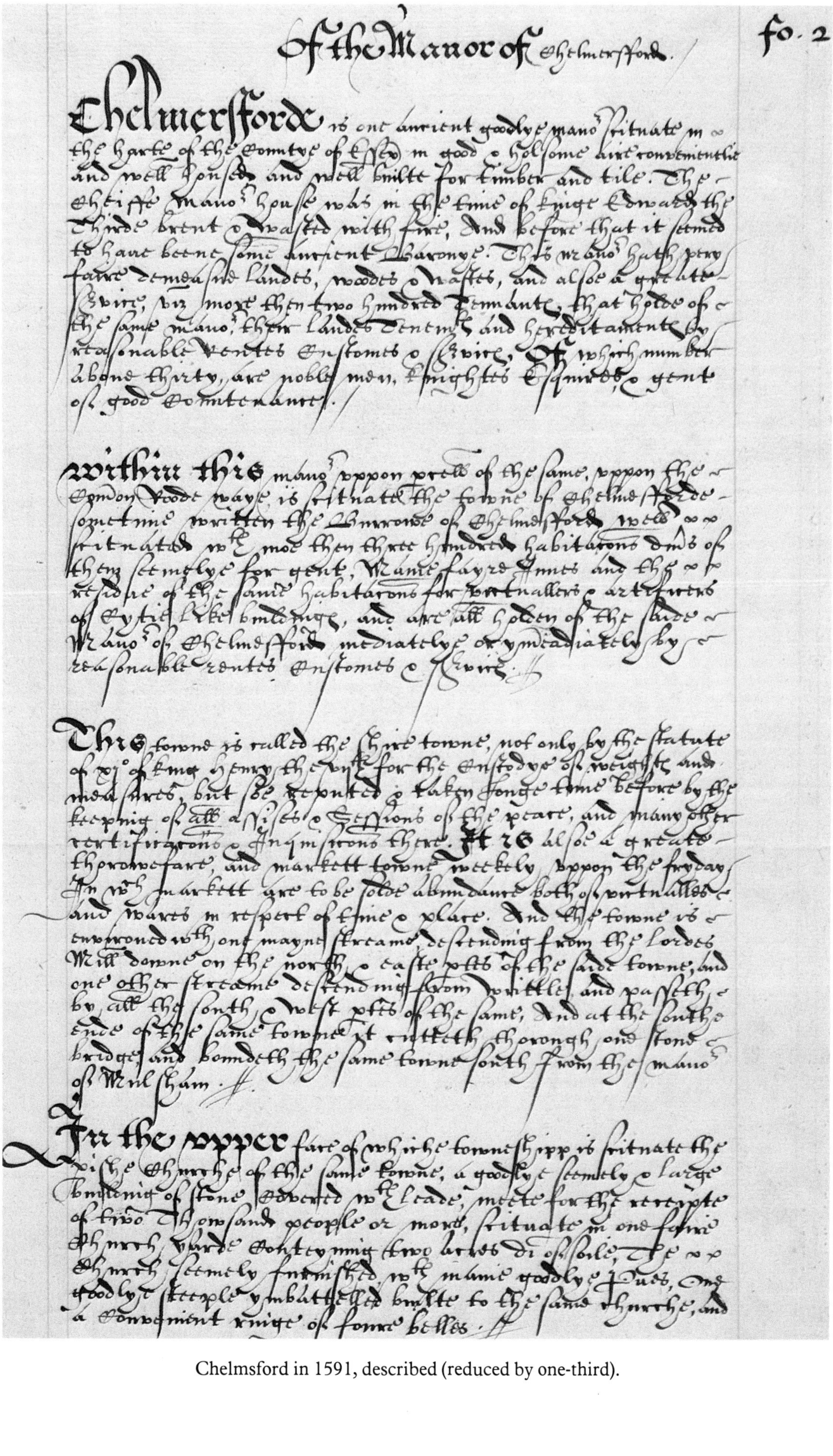

PLATE VI

Of the Manor of Chelmsford.

Chelmesford is one auncient goodlye manor situate in the harte of the Countye of Essex in good & holsome aire conuenientlie and well housed and well builte for timber and tile. The Chieffe Manor house was in the time of Kinge Edwarde the Thirde brent & wasted with fire, And before that it seemed to haue beene some auncient Baronye. This manor hath verye faire demeasne landes, woodes & pastes, and alsoe a greate Shire, viz more then two hundred Tennantes, that holde of the same manor, their landes, rentes and hereditamentes by reasonable rentes Customes & Seruice, Of which number aboue thirty, are noble men, Knightes Esquiers & gent of good Countenaunce.

Within this manor vppon parte of the same, vppon the London roade waye, is situate the towne of Chelmesforde sometime written the Burrowe of Chelmsforde well & — situated with moe then three hundred habitacions and of them seemlye for rent, manie faire Innes and the — residue of the same habitacions for vitnallers & artificers of sytie like knowledge, and are all holden of the saide Manor of Chelmesford mediatelye or ymediatelye by reasonable rentes Customes & Seruice.

This towne is called the Shire towne, not only by the statute of xj of Kinge Henry the vijth for the Custodye of weightes and measures, but soe reputed & taken longe time before by the keepinge of all assises & Sessions of the peace, and many other Certificacions & Inquisicions there. It is also a greate thorowefare, and markett towne weekely vppon the friday, In which markett are to be solde abundance both of vitnalles and wares in respect of the place. And the towne is enuironed with one maine streame, descendinge from the Lordes Mill downe on the north & easte pts of the saide towne, and one other streame descendinge from writtle and passeth by all the south & west pts of the same, And at the south ende of the same towne it rvnneth thorough one stone bridge and boundeth the same towne south from the manor of Mulsham.

In the vpper parte of which townshipp is situate the rich Churche of the same towne, a goodlye & seemlye & large buildinge of stone Couered with leade, meete for the receipte of two thowsand people or more, situate in one faire Churche yarde Conteyninge two acres di of soile, the — Church seemlye furnished with manie goodlye pues, one goodlye & steeple ymbattelled builte to the same Churche, and a Conuenient ringe of fowre belles.

PLATE VII

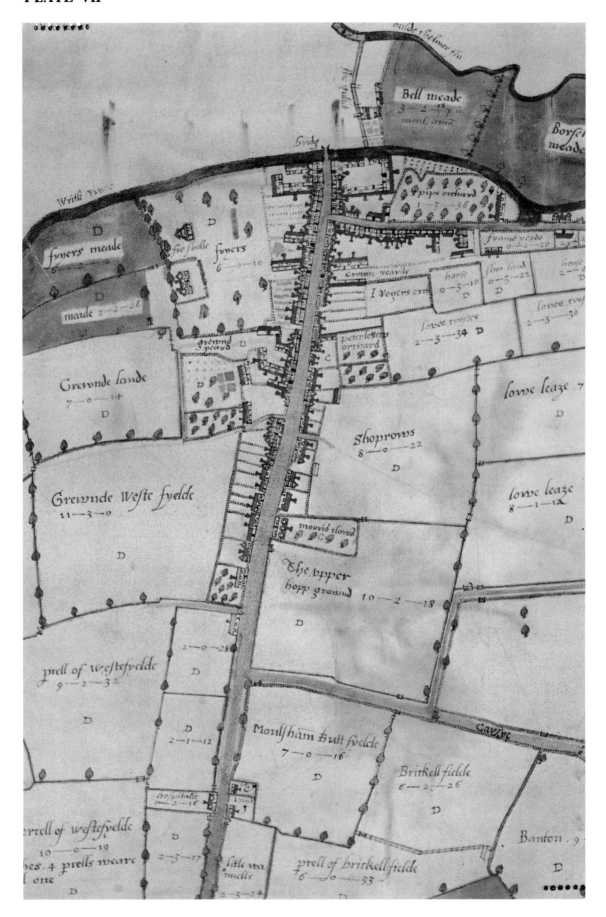

Moulsham Hamlet in 1591 (slightly reduced).

PLATE VIII

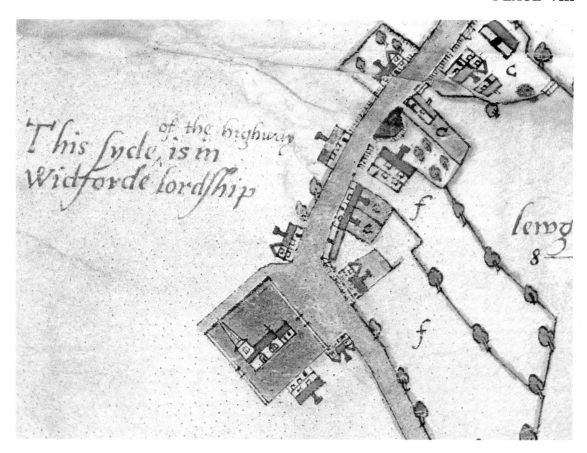

Widford Village in 1591 (slightly enlarged).

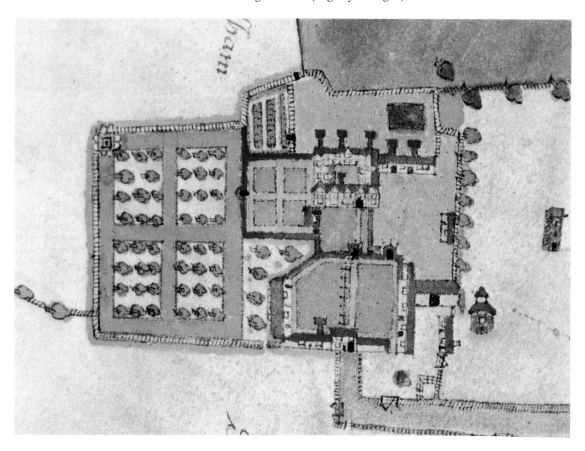

Moulsham Hall in 1591 (slightly enlarged).

PLATE IX

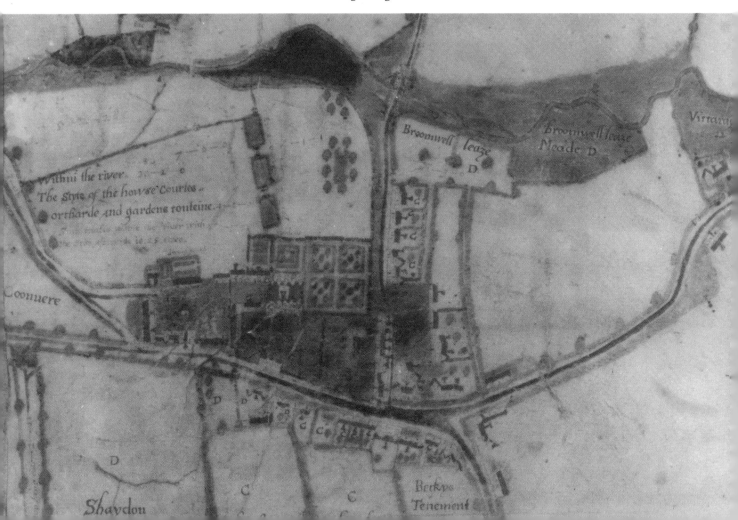

A brief survey of the demesne of the Manor of East West Hanningfield, 1592.

Terling Village in 1597.

PLATE X

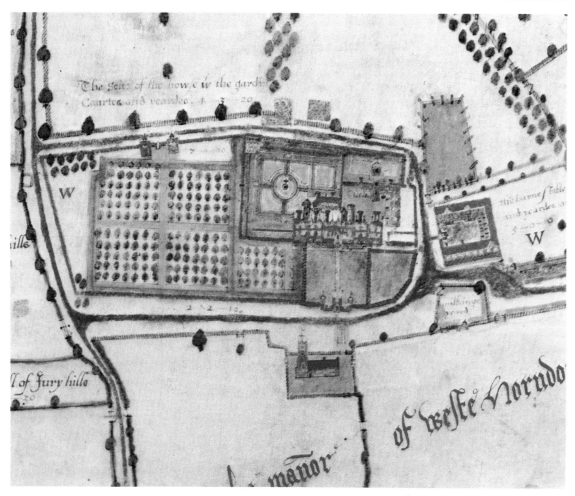

'Old' Thorndon Hall, 1598 (slightly reduced).

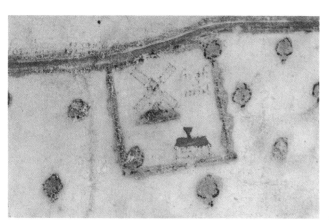

High Mill, West Horndon, 1598.

Mr. Waldegrave's Arbour, 1598.

PLATE XI

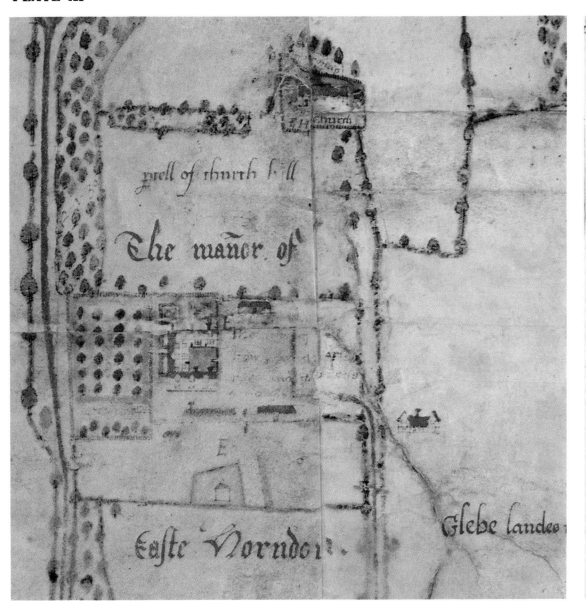

East Horndon Manor House and Church, 1598.

PLATE XII

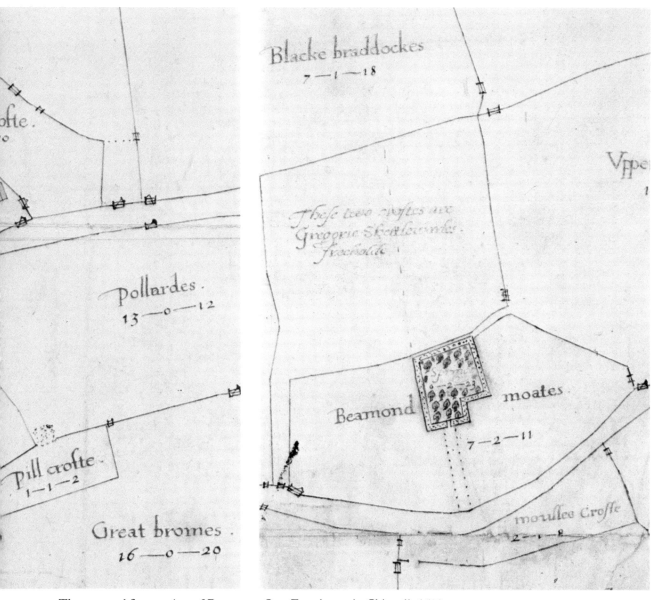

ofte.

Pollardes.
13 — 0 — 12

Pill crofte.
1 — 1 — 2

Great bromes.
16 — 0 — 20

Blacke braddockes
7 — 1 — 18

Vppe

Thefe two croftes are
Gregorie Shettleworkes
freehold

Beamond   moates
7 — 2 — 11

moulfes Crofte

The new and former sites of Beaumont Otes Farmhouse in Chignall, 1599.

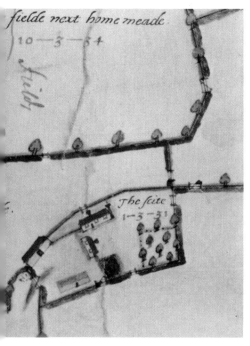

fielde next home meade.
10 — 3 — 34

field

The fcite
1 — 3 — 31

n Hall, Purleigh, 1600.

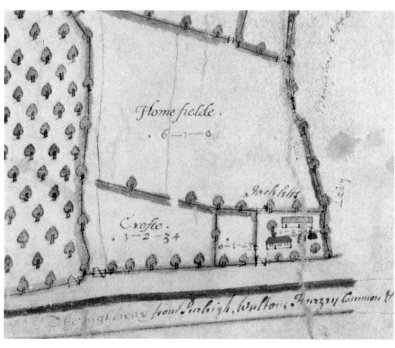

Home fielde.
6 — 1 — 0

Inch fitts

Crofte.
1 — 2 — 34

The highway from Purleigh, Walton, Runzey Common &

Jacklett's Farm, Danbury, c. 1600.

PLATE XIII

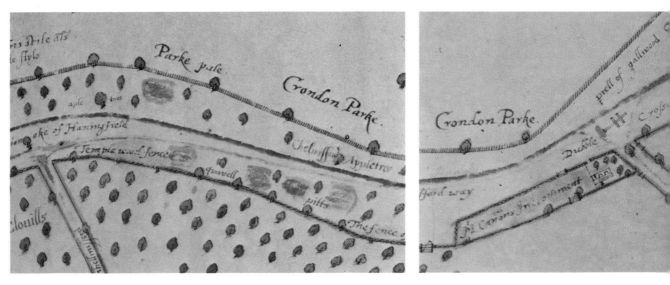

Extensive roadside waste at Stock and West Hanningfield, *c.* 1600 (reduced by one-quarter).

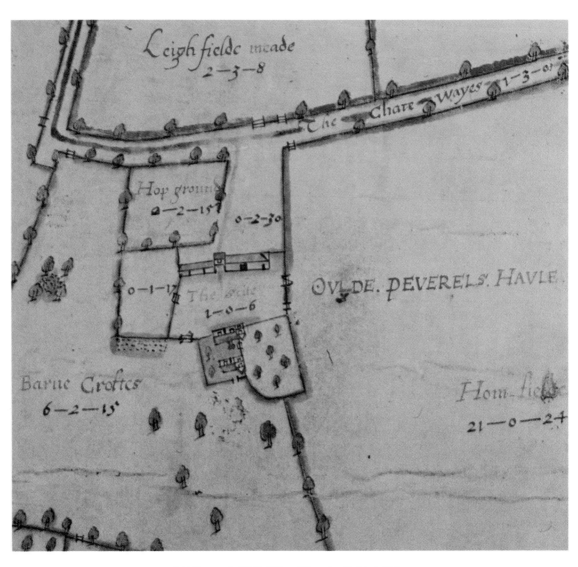

Old Peverels Hall, West Hanningfield, 1601.

PLATE XIV

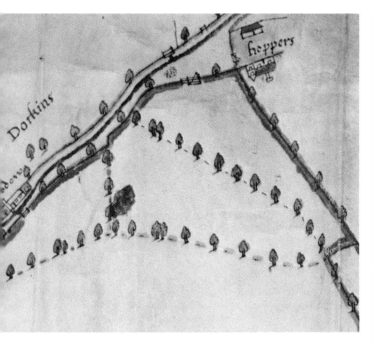

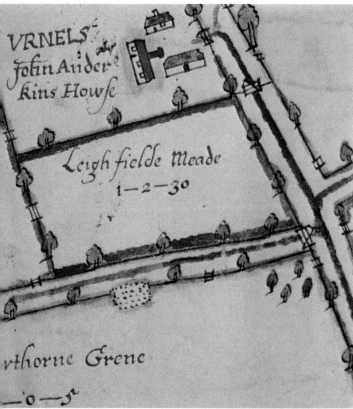

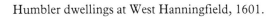

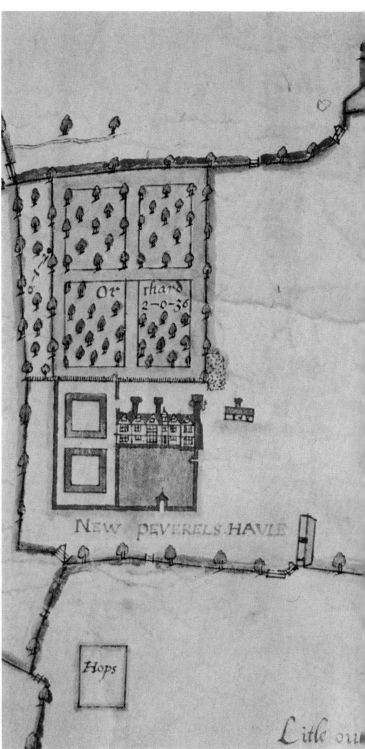

Humbler dwellings at West Hanningfield, 1601.

New Peverels Hall, West Hanningfield, 1601.

PLATE XV

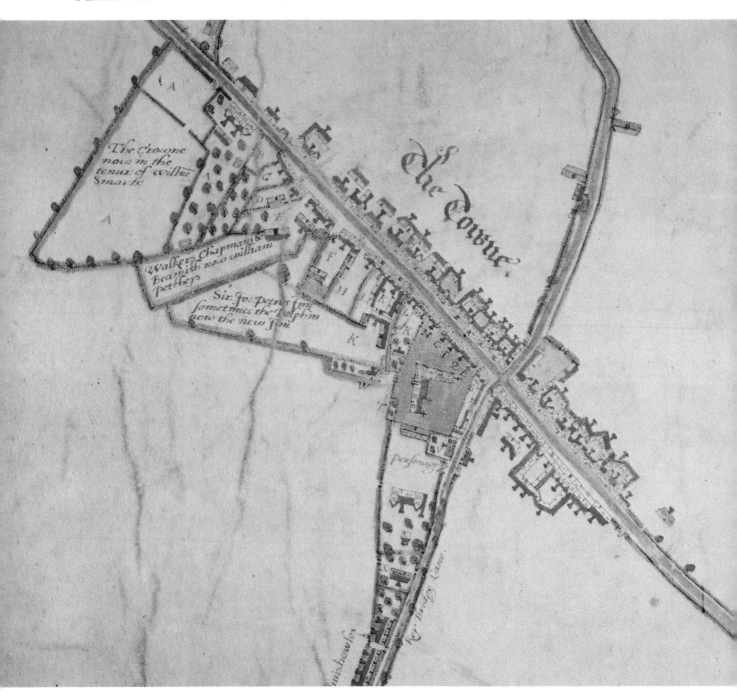

Ingatestone High Street in 1601.

PLATE XVI

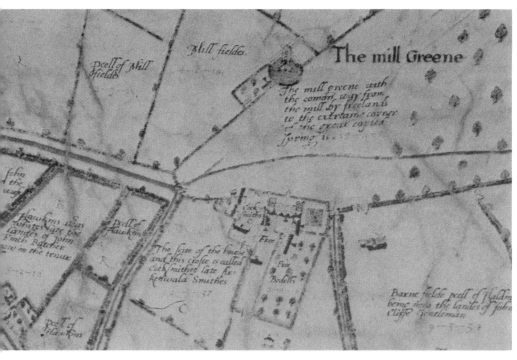

Mill Green, Ingatestone, 1601 (slightly reduced).

Kilns at Potter Row,
Ingatestone, 1601.

A survey of the Manor of Ingatestone, 1602, based on the Walker Map, 1601.

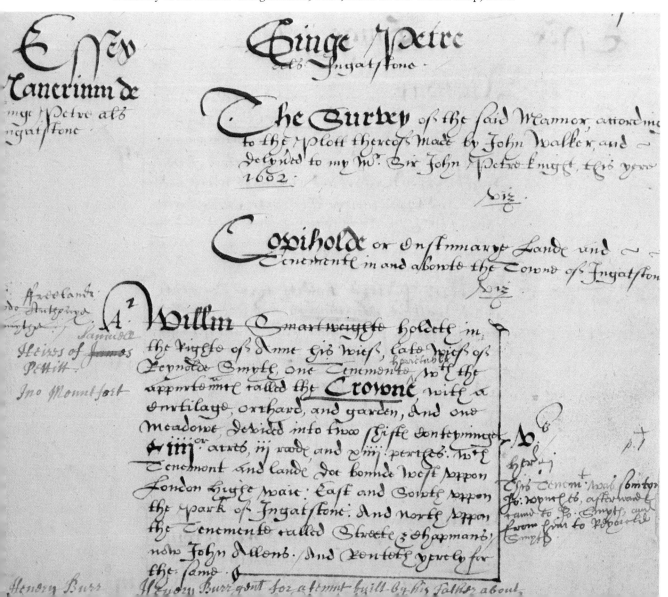

PLATE XVII

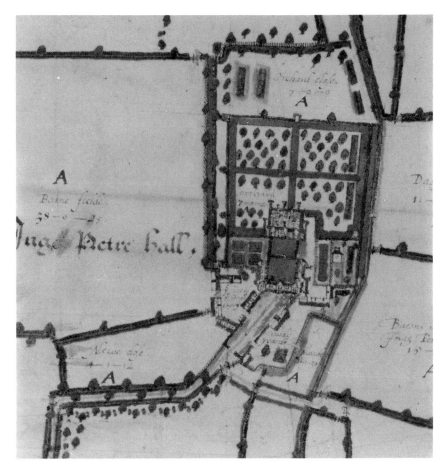

Ingatestone Hall, 1605.

Ingatestone High Street, 1605.

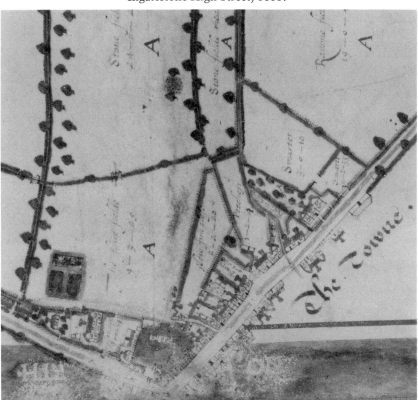

PLATE XVIII

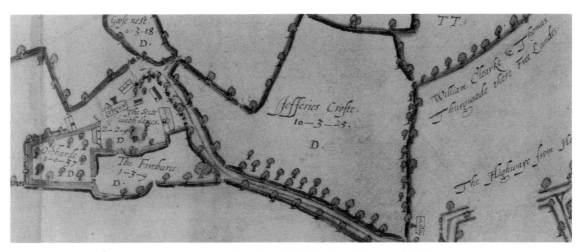

Housham Hall, Matching, 1609 (reduced by one-third).

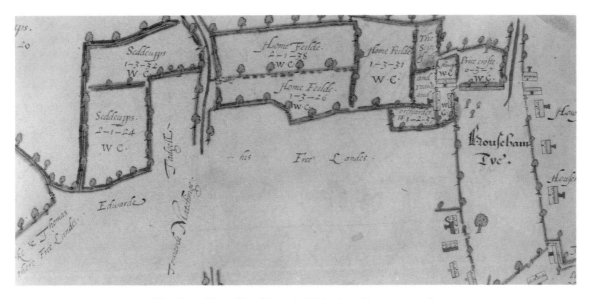

Housham Tye, Matching, 1609 (reduced by one-third).

Newman's End, Matching, 1609 (reduced by one-third).

PLATE XIX

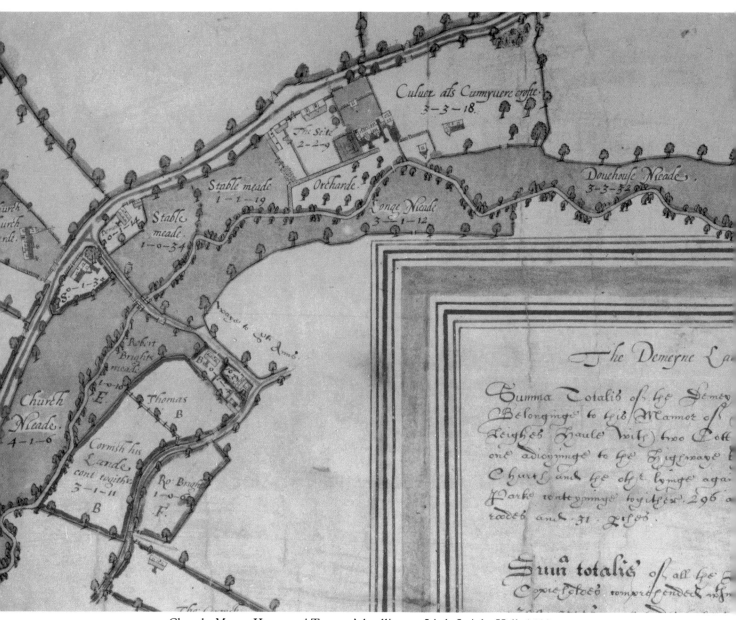

Church, Manor House and Tenants' dwellings at Little Leighs Hall, 1609.

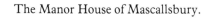

The Manor House of Mascallsbury.

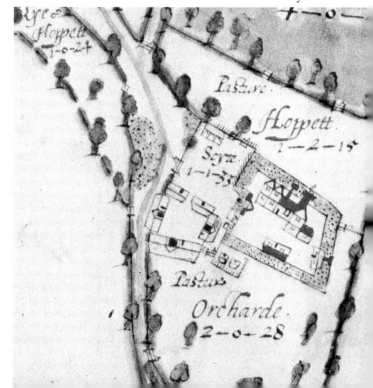

PLATE XX

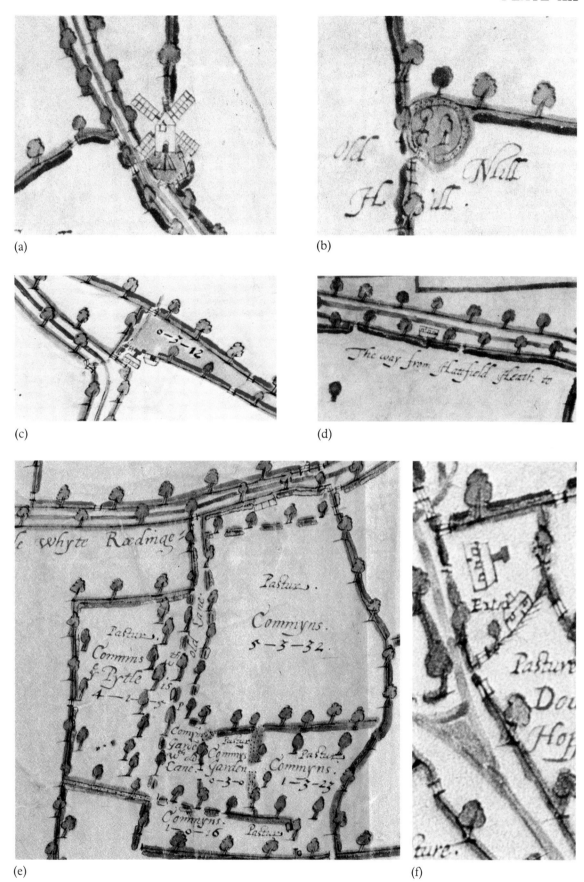

(a)

(b)

(c)

(d)

(e)

(f)

(a-f) Mill and Cottages at White Roothing, 1609.

PLATE XXI

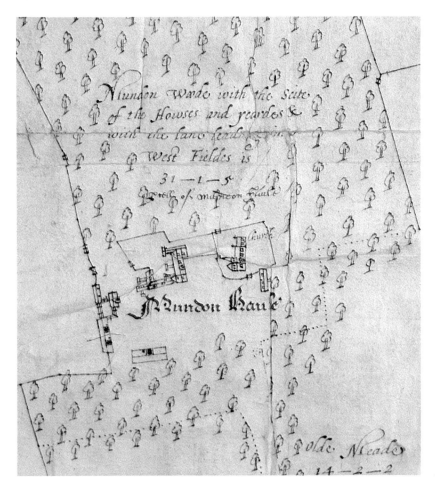

Mundon Hall, 1612.

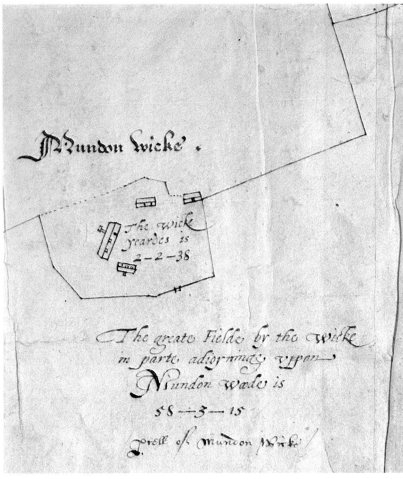

Wick Farm, Mundon, 1612.

PLATE XXII

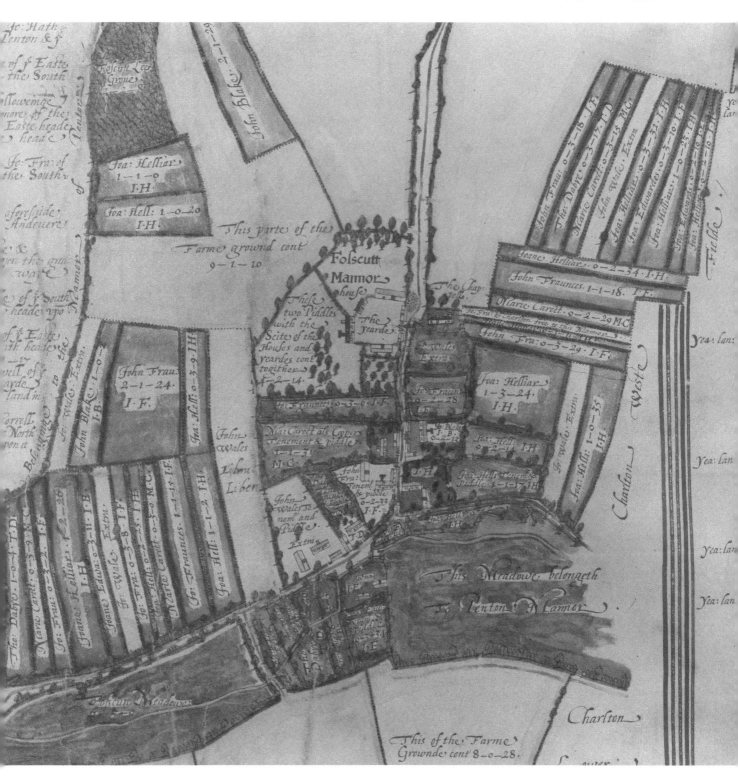

The Manor of Foxcott, Hampshire, 1614 (slightly reduced).

PLATE XXIII

A Surveye of the Free houldes houlden of the right Honourable the Lorde Burgaveneie of his aforesaide Manner of Easte Westhanningfielde.

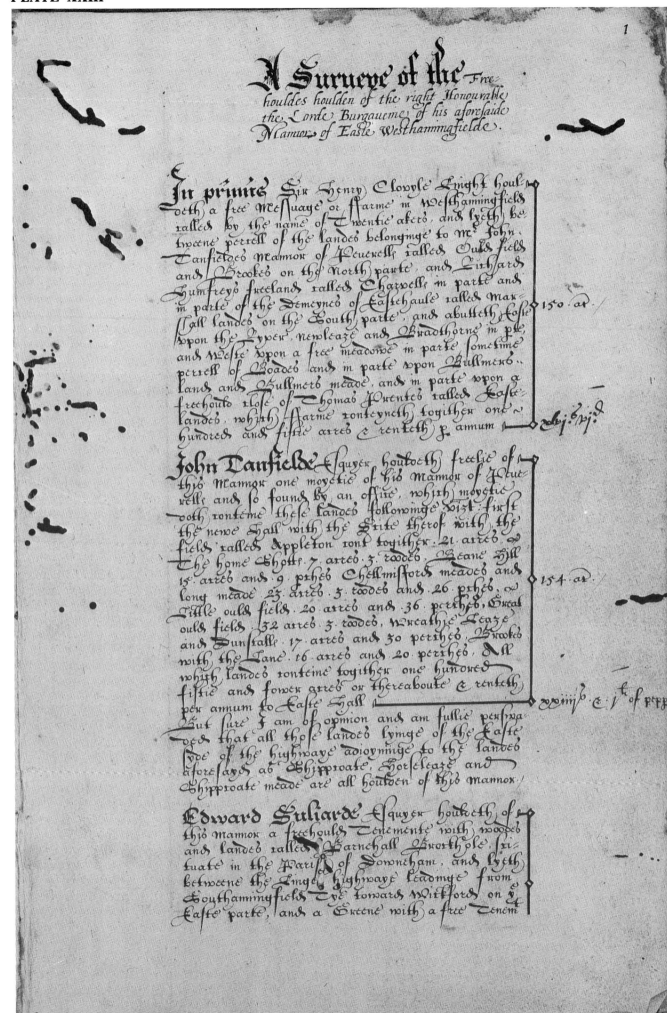

Imprimis Sir Henry Clovyle Knight houldeth a free Messuage or farme in Westhanningfield called by the name of twentie akers, and lyeth betweene perrell of the landes belonginge to Mr John Tanfieldes Mannor of Fouerell called Ould field and Brookes on the North parte, and Richard Humfreys freeland called Charwell in parte and in parte of the Demeynes of Castehaule called Marshall landes on the South parte, and abutteth Easte vpon the Vpper newleaze and Bradthorne in pte, and Weste vpon a free meadowe in parte sometime perrell of Boades and in parte vpon Bullmers land and Bullmers meade, and in parte vpon a freehould close of Thomas Wrentes called Eastelandes, which ffarme conteyneth togither one hundred and fiftie acres & renteth p' annum — 150 a' / ... xxij.ij.d

John Tanfielde Esquyer houldeth freelie of this Mannor one moyetie of his Mannor of Fouerell and so found by an office, which moyetie doth conteine these landes followinge viz: first the newe Hall with the Scite therof with the field called Appleton cont togither 21 acres, the home Shotts 7 acres 3 roodes, Beane Hill 15 acres and 9 pthes, Chellmisford meades and long meade 23 acres 3 roodes and 26 pthes, Little ould field 20 acres and 36 perches, Great ould field 32 acres 3 roodes, Wreathie Leaze and Dunstale 17 acres and 30 perches, Brookes with the Lane 16 acres and 20 perches, All which landes conteine togither one hundred fiftie and fower acres or thereaboute & renteth per annum to Caste Hall — 154 a' / ... xxiij.s & j.t of pepp

But sure I am of opinion and am fullie perswaded that all those landes lyinge of the Easte syde of the highwaye adioyninge to the landes aforesaid as Shipproate, horseleaze and Shipproate meade are all houlden of this mannor.

Edward Suliarde Esquyer houldeth of this mannor a freehould tenemente with woodes and landes called Barnehall Brorthple, sc' tuate in the Parish of Downeham, and lyeth betweene the Kinges highwaye leadinge from Southanninyfield Tye towarde Wikford on the Easte parte, and a Greene with a free tenem'

PLATE XXIV

The Hamlet of East Hanningfield Tye, 1615.

PLATE XXV

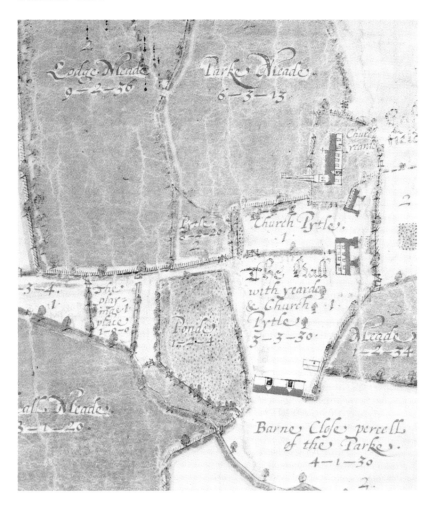

East Hanningfield Hall
and Church, 1615.

West Hanningfield Church
and its surroundings, 1615.

PLATE XXVI

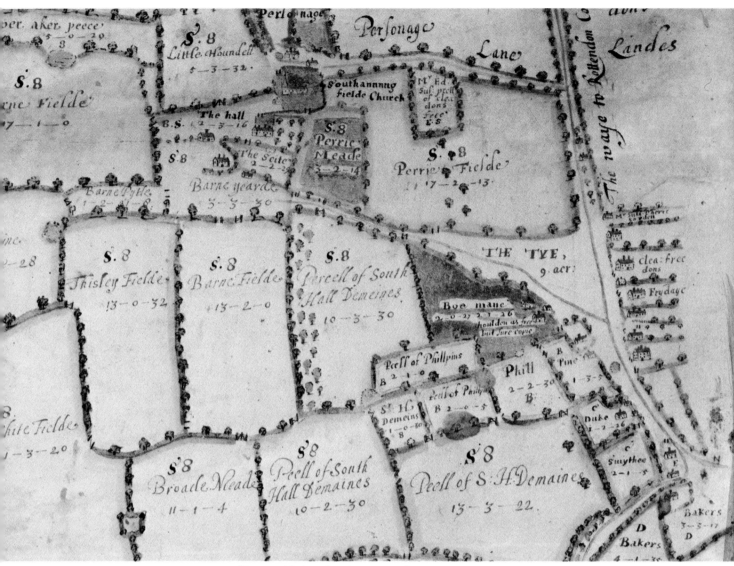

Above and below: South Hanningfield, *c.*1615.

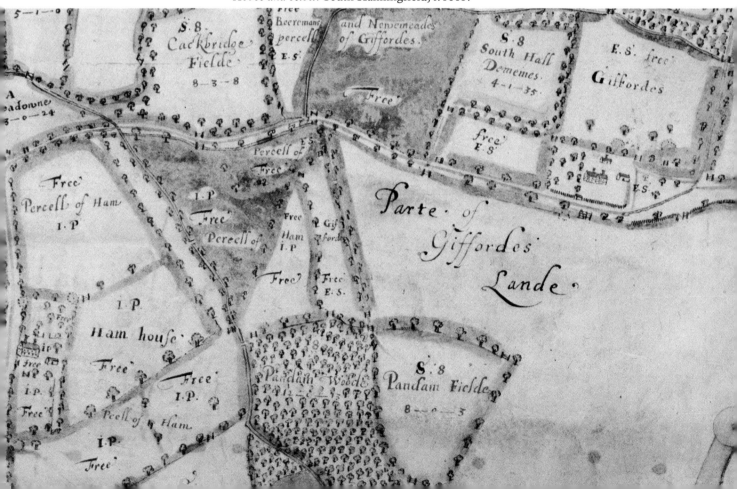

PLATE XXVII

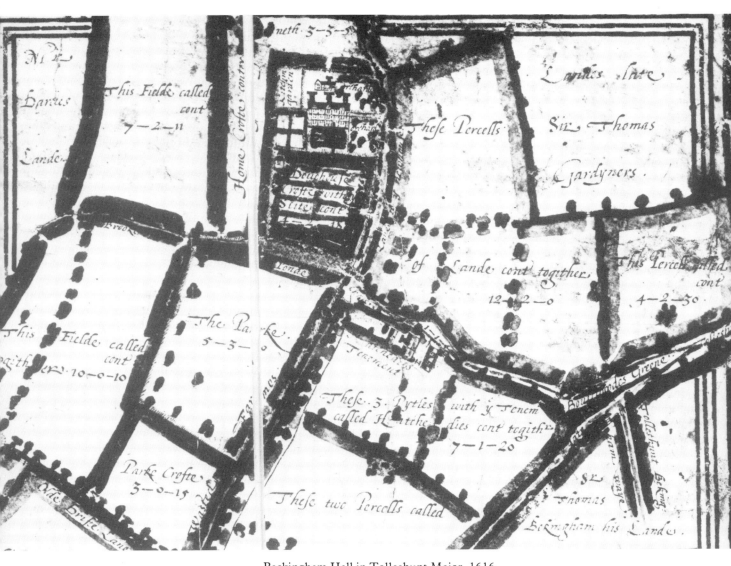

Beckingham Hall in Tolleshunt Major, 1616.

Buttsbury Church, 1616.

Church and dwellings at Stock, 1616.

PLATE XXVIII

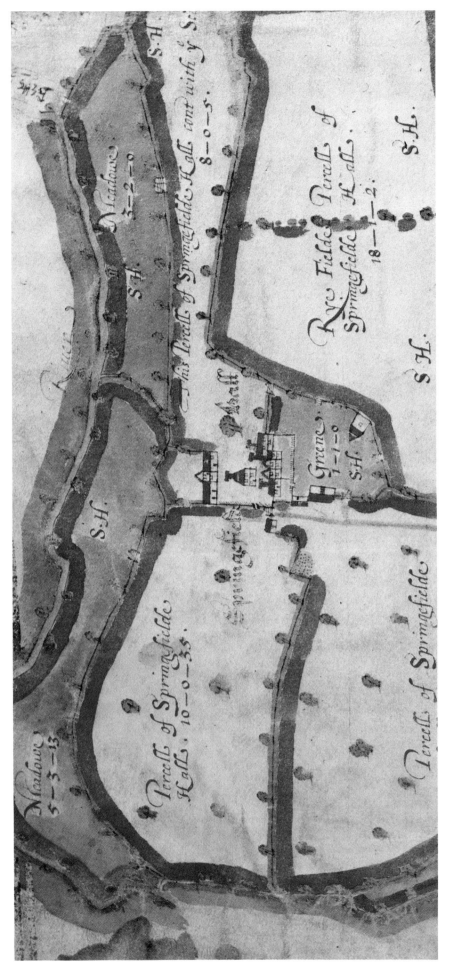

Springfield Hall,
*c.*1616.

PLATE XXIX

Springfield Village, *c.* 1616.

PLATE XXX

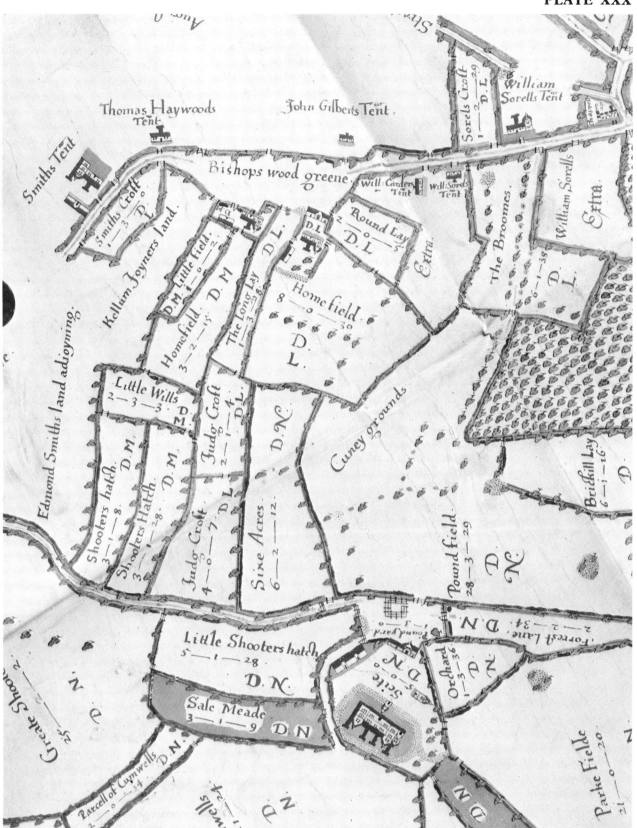

High Easter, 1622

PLATE XXXI

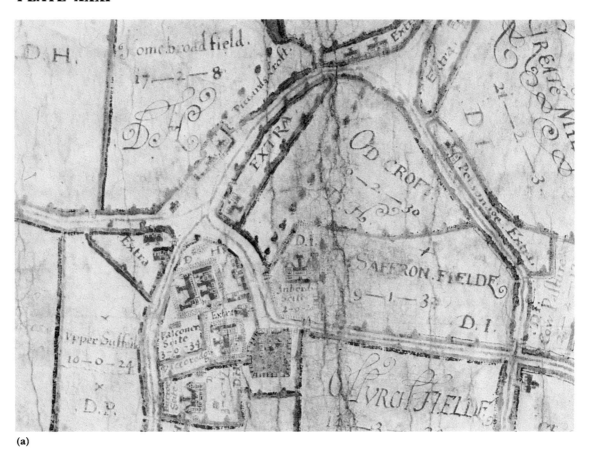

(a)

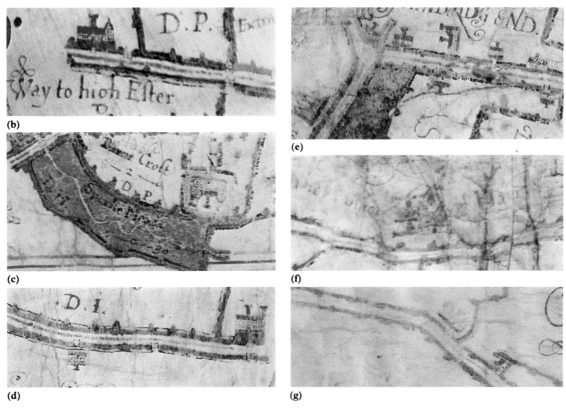

(b)

(c)

(d)

(e)

(f)

(g)

(a-g) Dwellings at Good Easter, 1623.

PLATE XXXII

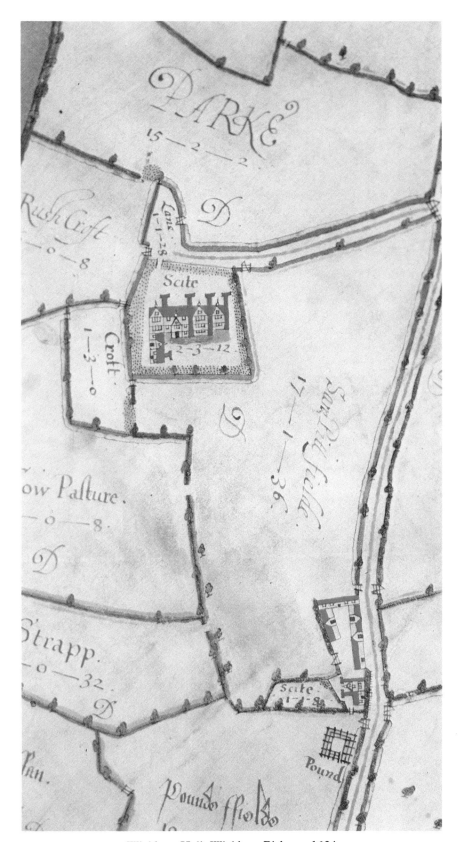

Wickham Hall, Wickham Bishops, 1624.

PLATE XXXIII

Richard Loane [holdeth] One Cottage neere the
three Elmes [called] Greenes Late Mathew Loanes And
£ [Lyeth] North-West on the Kinges highway Leadinge
2 from Westhanningfield Church to Stock. And
abutteth South vpon A Capitall Messuage [called]
Helmans on the Greene. Conteyninge One Roode
and Eight Perches. [And holdeth] Per Annum a

9.

ii.d ob.

John Younge [holdeth] One Customarie Parcell
[called] Powlens. Somtimes John Bowens. Late Thomas
Rams. And [lyeth] betweene the Kings Highway leadinge
£ from Westhanningfield Church toward Chelmesforde
3 And [Lyeth] North on A Customarie farme [called]
Helman on the hill. And side West on A Free
Tennement of the [sayd] John Youngs [called] Bowins
And [sydeth] East on A Coppie peece of land [called]
Millfielde. Conteyninge three Acres And Twentie
foure Perches. And [holdeth] a

viij.d

And One
Heriott /

Richard Humfrey [holdeth] One Capitall Messuage
or farme Customary Called by these Severall names. being
but One intire thinge. [Viz] Helman on the Greene.
westborne-land. Cullins; Hobbs-lande. Hobbes
groue. Butt-field. and Powlens als Powlers [these]
£ lands being Late Richard Cannons. And lieth betweene The
50 Kings high Way leading from Westhanningfield Church to
Chelmesford on [y] North in parte And [yet] on a tenement called Oliuers
now Stephen Hamkins. And parte on the Parsonage of Westhanningfield And South on [y] Lands of Henry Clowte called Pynnings
in [parte]: And [yet] on a [prcell] of Glebe called Crowland. And abuttinge
East vpon A Messuage of Freeland called Parrages in parte: And [yet]
on a meade Coppie of [y] said Richard Humfreys called Mother Westers meade
And lieth West on another highway leading from the Three Elmes to
South-hanningfield Tye. Conteyninge Eighty fiue Acres: and three Roodes
And [holdeth] Per Annum to the Lord a

iij.li xij.s vij.d ob.

And One
Heriott /

The same

From the survey of the Hanningfield Manors, 1628.
(slightly reduced)

PLATE XXXIV

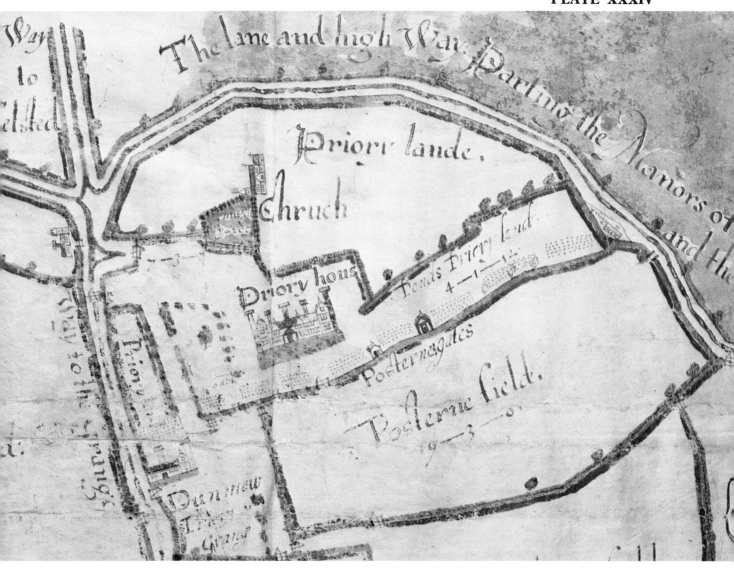

Little Dunmow Priory, 1631.

Mountnessing Hall, 1622.

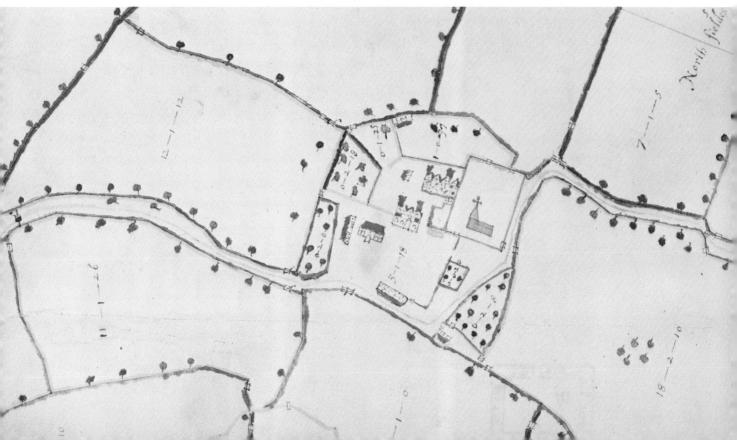

PLATE XXXV

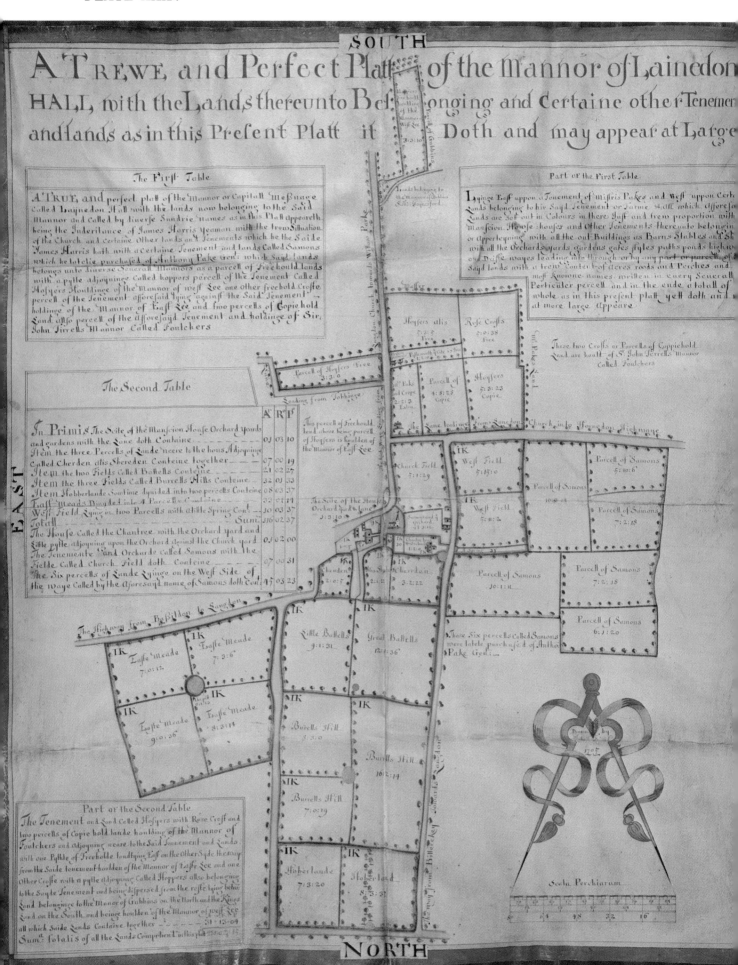

Laindon Hall, dated 1705, but obviously a copy of a lost Walker map, c. 1600.

(a)

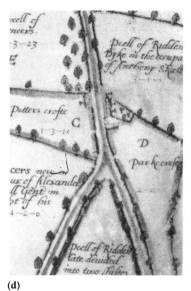

(b)

(d)

(c)

(e)

(f)

(g)

PLATE XXXVII

Haldins, Ingatestone, 1601.

Haldins, now Hardings Farm.

Boxted—Dolf's Cottage
This building, like Vine Cottage,
is depicted on Walker's map of 1586.

PLATE XXXVIII

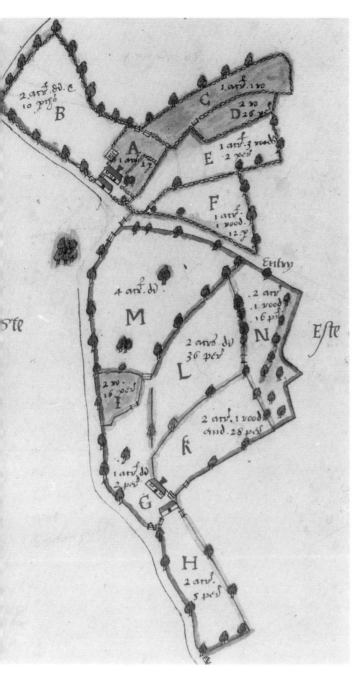

Boxted, 1586.
The building now known as
Vine Cottage, is marked 'G'
on the map.

Boxted—Vine Cottage today
General view of cottage.

Vine Cottage showing central crown
post of hall and other roof timbers
(behind modern timber).

PLATE XXXIX

Housham Hall, Matching.

Housham Hall,
Matching, the larger barn.

Housham Hall,
Matching, the smaller barn.

House at Housham Tye.

Kents Farm,
West Hanningfield,
the Walkers home.